VICTORIOUS CHRISTIANS YOU SHOULD KNOW

VICTORIOUS CHRISTIANS
You Should Know

WARREN W. WIERSBE

Baker Book House

Grand Rapids, Michigan 49506

Contents

1. Readers Are Leaders   7
2. Servant of an Illustrious Master   11
3. "Beaten Oil" and McCheyne   16
4. Fanny Crosby—Blind to See God   22
5. Millionaire Missionary   27
6. Fanny Crosby's British Counterpart   35
7. Bonar—Minister with the Laughing Face   41
8. The Preacher Who Couldn't Preach   48
9. The Apostle of the Haphazard   53
10. Aristocrat in the Pulpit   60
11. One-Eyed Preacher from the North   68
12. Apostle of Certainty   74
13. George Whitefield—Assistant to All   81
14. Everybody's Expositor   89
15. Martin Luther's Rib   95
16. Missionary Unpredictable   102
17. Jonathan Edwards—Brilliant Mind, Burning Heart   110
18. Samuel Chadwick—A Burning and Shining Light   118
19. Bishop with a Bible   125

1

Readers Are Leaders

The next time you pick up any English translation of the Bible, give thanks to God for the life and ministry of William Tyndale (1494–1536). It was Tyndale who paved the way for the translation of the Bible from the original languages into English, and this ministry cost him his life.

The difficulties Tyndale had to overcome to get his work done were colossal. He experienced shipwreck. His precious manuscripts were lost. The established church hounded and persecuted him, and secret agents were constantly after him. The police even raided the printshop where his translation was being published. Some of his "friends" betrayed him. Tyndale was arrested in 1535 in Belgium, and in 1536 he was strangled and burned at the stake.

My reason for citing these facts is to pave the way for a quotation from one of the letters Tyndale wrote while he was in prison:

> I entreat your lordship, and that by the Lord Jesus, that if I must remain here for the winter you would beg the Commissary to be so kind as to send me, from the things of mine which he has, a warmer cap; I feel the cold painfully in my head. Also a warmer cloak, for the cloak I have is very thin. He has a woollen

shirt of mine, if he will send it. But most of all, My Hebrew
Bible, Grammar, and Vocabulary, that I may spend my time in
that pursuit.

Every reader of the Bible will immediately associate this
request with one which the Apostle Paul made to his beloved
son in the faith, Timothy. "The cloak that I left at Troas with
Carpus, when thou comest, bring with thee, and the books, but
especially the parchments" (II Tim. 4:13).

We have no idea what these books were that Paul urgently
requested, but we do know that they were important to him.
It is possible that portions of the Old Testament Scriptures
were among them. At any rate, it is worth noting that both
Paul and Tyndale requested books as their companions as they
awaited trial and certain death.

Charles Spurgeon had a marvelous comment on Paul's
request:

> He is inspired, yet he wants books! He has been preaching
> at least for 30 years, yet he wants books! He has seen the Lord,
> and yet he wants books! He has had a wider experience than
> most men, yet he wants books! He had been caught up into the
> third heaven, and had heard things which it is unlawful for a
> man to utter, yet he wants books! He had written the major
> part of the New Testament, yet he wants books!

How I wish that this same desire for good books character-
ized more believers today!

Some years ago, an American paper manufacturing company ran a series of ads in the major magazines, and each one
had the same caption: "Send us a man who reads!" In recent
years, the slogan Readers are Leaders! has appeared in many
places. Somehow, these messages have not gotten through to
some of God's people. One purpose of this book is to encourage
our readers to invest their time in reading good books.

After all, reading is to the mind what eating is to the body:
it provides nourishment. I read somewhere, "The mind grows
by what it takes in, and the heart grows by what it gives out."

Many people are starving their minds by neglecting the nutritious volumes that are available for their reading. They try to minister to others, but they have nothing to give.

Our God is a God of truth. "He is the Rock, his work is perfect . . . a God of truth and without iniquity" (Deut. 32:4). God put truth into creation and thus made possible science and engineering. His Son is named "the truth" (see John 14:6); and the Holy Spirit is "the Spirit of truth" (v. 17). We never have to fear truth because all truth comes from God and leads to God. "Thy word is truth" (17:17). God can write his truth in the skies (Ps. 19:1–6) or in the Scriptures (vv. 7–11), and there will be no contradiction.

God made man to appreciate and use truth. He gave us a mind to think with, and he expects us to use it. God puts no premium on ignorance, even though he warns us against trusting the wisdom of the world. Years ago, when I was a young Christian heading for college, Dr. Torrey Johnson advised me, "Learn all you can, put it under the blood, and use it for Jesus' sake." I have tried to follow that wise counsel and share it with others.

We must face the fact that *God* wrote a book—*the Bible*. We must also face the fact that he gave teachers to the church (see Eph. 4:11), and that "apt to teach" is one of the important qualifications for a pastor (I Tim. 3:2). Of course apt to teach implies apt to learn. Yet many pastors, sad to say, do not read and, as a consequence, they do not grow. This means that their people do not grow and that the church does not prosper. "You have a fine library," I said to a pastor who had invited me to minister in his pulpit. "Yes," he replied, "and I wish I had time to use it."

Reading is not a matter of having time, but of taking time, of making time. We always make time for the things that are important to us. God gives each of us twenty-four hours a day, and how we use those hours reveals the priorities in our lives. If you devoted only thirty minutes a day to serious reading, you could complete the average book in at least a week. I always carry books with me when I travel (you could write a

book waiting for some planes to take off), and when I make
my visits to the doctor or dentist or anywhere else that might
involve a wait. I would rather read a good Christian book than
the ancient magazines in the doctor's office!

"But, I'm just not the student type!" someone may argue.
I'm not sure I know what the student type is. You can be sure
that I am not encouraging anybody to become an ivory-tower
recluse, a bookworm who isolates himself from life and reads
himself into senility. There is no such thing as the student
type, because all kinds of people enjoy reading. Many readers
of this book are serious Bible students, and that in itself proves
that they can handle books; for a knowledge of the Bible is
more important than a college education. If you have learned
to use your Bible, you can master any other book.

No, the time has come for us to lay aside our feeble excuses
and come to grips with the serious business of reading for
learning and living. Never underestimate the power of a book.
According to one authority, for every word in Hitler's *Mein
Kampf*, 125 lives were lost in World War II.

What shall we read? Certainly the Bible and books that help
us understand it better. We also need to read books that will
help us serve the Lord better. But along with these we must
also read books that will help us build our lives and our
homes—biographies of great Christians, the classics that have
endured the test of time, and those mind-stretching books that
we have always avoided.

One of my purposes here is to introduce you to the best in
Christian reading, to encourage you to go to your own book-
shelf, the church library, or your nearest Christian bookstore,
or perhaps borrow from a friend that one book you have always meant to read—and start reading it!

Remember, readers are leaders.

2

Servant of
an Illustrious Master

The only thing that the almanac lists for May 21, 1832, is "First National Democratic Convention meets in Baltimore." But then, almanacs never record the spiritual side of history. On that date, James Hudson Taylor was born in Barnsley, Yorkshire, England; and James Hudson Taylor was the man God used to found the China Inland Mission (now the Overseas Missionary Fellowship) and to bring the gospel to lost sinners in inland China.

The story is recorded in *God's Man in China*, by Dr. and Mrs. Howard Taylor, the son and daughter-in-law of Hudson Taylor. Published by Moody Press, this volume is a popular edition of *The Biography of James Hudson Taylor*, published in 1965 by the China Inland Mission to help commemorate their centenary. In turn, this volume is an abridgment of the large two-volume work, *Hudson Taylor in Early Years* and *Hudson Taylor and the China Inland Mission*. The two-volume work is difficult to find these days; so if you locate a set, hold on to it—and read it. But the one-volume abridgment contains the heart of the history of this remarkable man and the mission that he founded.

Unlike some missionary biographies that tend to glorify men, all these volumes major on magnifying God. In his own brief autobiography, *A Retrospect* (Moody Press, now out of print), Taylor wrote: "It is always helpful to us to fix our attention on the Godward aspect of Christian work; to realize that the work of God does not mean so much man's work for God, as God's own work through man" (pp. 7–8).

What were the influences that God brought to bear upon Hudson Taylor to make him the spiritual giant that he was?

At the top of the list must be *a spiritual home.* Taylor's father was a lay evangelist and his mother a woman of prayer. In fact, unknown to the family, Taylor's father had begun to pray for the land of China two years before his son was born. The lad's conversion, when he was about fifteen, came as the result of the prayers of his mother and his sister. The family honored the Bible and prayer and sought to honor Christ in everything. "Brought up in such a circle and saved under such circumstances," Taylor wrote in later years, "It was perhaps natural that from the beginning of my Christian life I was led to feel that the promises were very real, and that prayer was a sober matter-of-fact transacting business with God, whether on one's own behalf or on behalf of those for whom one sought His blessing" (*A Retrospect,* p. 13).

Perhaps the next influence was *the sense of a definite call from God.* In our day, teenagers are not expected to get serious about God's will for their lives, and our churches and missions are suffering as a result (I have preached in Christian schools and met far too many students who did not know why they were in school, let alone what God wanted them to do with their lives.) Only a few months after his conversion, Hudson Taylor dared to seek God's will for his life. "I besought Him to give me some work to do for Him . . . something with which He would be pleased, and that I might do for Him who had done so much for me." As an act of faith, he totally consecrated himself to the Lord. "I remember stretching myself on the ground, and lying there silent before Him with unspeakable awe and unspeakable joy" (*A Retrospect,* pp. 14, 15).

A few minutes later, he felt the distinct impression that God wanted him to be a missionary to China. He then borrowed a book on China from a Congregational minister in town, who asked him how he proposed to go to China. Taylor replied that, like the apostles of old, he intended to trust God for all his needs. "Ah, my boy, as you grow older," said the minister, "you will get wiser than that." But that was the very policy that Taylor followed all his life and ministry, and God honored it. Neither he nor the mission promoted for funds. They prayed and trusted God to raise up friends who would, constrained by God, share their means and help to meet the needs.

This leads us to a third influence: *God prepared Hudson Taylor at home.* Before he sailed for China, Taylor practiced the principles of sacrifice and service, trusting God to meet all his needs. He did away with all material comforts; he exercised; he lived on a plain diet; he economized. As a result, he had extra funds to share with others, and he learned how to do without. After all, if he could not learn to trust God at home, where life was easy, how could he ever learn to trust God in a difficult place like China?

I once met a young couple in London who told me they were from Florida. "Are you visiting Europe?" I asked.

"Oh, no! We're missionaries" they replied. "We've come over here to start new churches."

I asked, "Have you ever started any new churches in America?" It turned out that they had never started a new church anywhere. I felt that they were totally unprepared to serve as missionaries, and I wondered that their mission board permitted them to serve.

God's Man in China gives one exciting account after another of God's preparation of Hudson Taylor before he left Britain. Taylor learned to pray and trust God for finances. He learned to give what he had to others, trusting God to meet his needs a day at a time. His faith in God, and sober living, saved his life when he contracted blood poisoning while in medical training in London. I wonder how many missionaries or pastors today have permitted God to train them in this way. And as for disciplined living, the least said about this among believers, the better.

As you read *God's Man in China*, you will be impressed with another influence in Taylor's life: *a love for all God's people and a desire for wide usefulness*. He did not promote the China Inland Mission; he promoted missions. If after he spoke, people contributed to other missionary projects, he was just as pleased as if the money had gone to CIM ministries. If believers surrendered their lives to serve Christ through other missions, he did not complain. His constant prayer was, "Lord, give me wide usefulness!" What a refreshing attitude this is in our day of competitive promotion among Christian ministries.

Finally, Hudson Taylor *depended wholly on the Lord*. You will read his experience in chapters 15 and 16 of the biography. The expanded version (and you must read it) is *Hudson Taylor's Spiritual Secret* (Moody Press). He discovered "the exchanged life" and entered into a relationship with Christ that took the wear and tear out of Christian service and replaced feverish activity with calm and joyful ministry. I try to read *Hudson Taylor's Spiritual Secret* once each year, and it always refreshes me. There are many academic theological explanations of the deeper life or the victorious life; but I think the experience of Hudson Taylor explains it best. It was not something that he manufactured, but something he experienced in his own life. No cute formulas, no clever outlines; just a personal and practical experience with Christ that any believer can enjoy.

In a very real sense, Hudson Taylor was a product of the ministry of John Wesley. Taylor's great-grandparents, James and Betty Taylor, were converted through the Wesleyan Revival, and even had the privilege of entertaining John Wesley in their humble Barnsley cottage. And Wesley had been brought to the assurance of salvation through the hearing of Luther's preface to his commentary on Romans. And Luther had been greatly influenced by John Tauler, the German Dominican mystic, who, in turn, had been influenced by Meister Eckhart, a leading German mystic. Let those who wish to confine the work of God to their own fellowships note and take heed.

Whenever people tried to praise Taylor for what he had done, he would simply reply, "All God's giants have been weak men, who did great things for God because they reckoned on His being with them." Once in Australia, he was introduced as "our illustrious guest"; and he said, "Dear friends, I am the little servant of an illustrious master." Perhaps in our own day we have too many celebrities and not enough servants.

Three Scripture texts must always be associated with James Hudson Taylor. The first is Mark 11:22—"Have faith in God." But to Taylor, this faith was not a blind hope that God would act. It was not superstition. He first sought the will of God, through prayer and study of the word; and then he committed the matter to the Lord and trusted him to work. "We have no responsibility save to follow as we are led," said Taylor, "and we serve One who is able both to design and to execute, and whose work never fails" (*God's Man in China*, p. 271).

The second text is I Samuel 7:12—"Ebenezer . . . Hitherto hath the Lord helped us." I note that some modern hymnals have dropped the word "Ebenezer" in the song "Come, Thou Fount of Every Blessing." It is another sad reminder of the growing biblical illiteracy of church members.

His third text was Genesis 22:14—"Jehovah-jireh . . . the Lord will provide" (literally, "the Lord will see to it"). Taylor had the two words *Ebenezer* and *Jehovah-jireh* inscribed on plaques which he always kept on the mantle wherever he was residing. "Have faith in God" was inscribed over one of the entrances of the CIM office in London.

Hudson Taylor died in China on June 3, 1905, and was buried at Chinkiang. Among his last words were: "There is nothing small, and there is nothing great: only God is great, and we should trust Him fully."

One of his co-laborers, J. W. Stevenson, said, "Oh, his was a life that stood looking into—searching through and through!" I urge Christians today to get acquainted with James Hudson Taylor and the principles of ministry that governed his life and work. They differ radically from the Madison Avenue ideas that seem to have captured some ministries. But his principles were tried and proved: they worked for Hudson Taylor, and they can work for us today.

3

Beaten Oil and McCheyne

"It is not great talents God blesses so much as great likenesses to Jesus. A holy minister is an awful weapon in the hand of God."

Those words were written on October 2, 1840, by Robert Murray McCheyne, pastor of St. Peter's Church, Dundee, Scotland. They are typical of McCheyne, for "likeness to Jesus" was the emphasis of his life and ministry. "I heard you preach last Sabbath evening," a stranger wrote him, "and it pleased God to bless that sermon to my soul. It was not so much what you said, as your manner of speaking that struck me. I saw in you a beauty in holiness that I never saw before."

I wonder if this "beauty of holiness" is not a missing ingredient in ministry today. We hear people boasting that their pastor is a good expositor (and there is nothing wrong with that), a good counselor, a man who is "fun to be with"; but we rarely hear people say, "Our pastor is a holy man of God." The people in Dundee could say that of McCheyne.

Robert Murray McCheyne was born in Edinburgh, Scotland, on May 21, 1813. His family discovered early that he was a precocious child: at the age of four, while recovering from an illness, he learned the Greek alphabet and was able to write the letters on his slate. He entered Edinburgh University in November. 1827, still an unconverted youth. The death of his brother David in 1831 stirred him deeply, and as a result he trusted Christ. That year, McCheyne entered the Divinity Hall and dedicated himself to the ministry of the Gospel. One of his fellow students, Andrew A. Bonar, became his close friend; and it is Bonar who, in 1844, published *The Memoirs and Remains of Robert Murray McCheyne,* today recognized as a great Christian classic.

He was licensed by the Presbytery (along with Andrew Bonar) on July 1, 1835; and the following November, he began his ministry as an assistant in the church at Larbert, near Stirling. From the very outset of his ministry, he threw himself in total dependence upon the Lord. He fed himself daily on the Word of God, and each Lord's Day would share his spiritual nourishment with the congregation. "I see a man cannot be a faithful minister, until he preaches Christ for Christ's sake," he wrote in his journal, "until he gives up striving to attract people to himself, and seeks only to attract them to Christ." We wonder what McCheyne would think of all the so-called Christian celebrities we have today—and the people who run after them.

On August 14, 1836, McCheyne was asked to candidate at a new extension church that had been opened in May in Dundee (Andrew Bonar was also a candidate). The population of Dundee had grown in recent years to more than fifty thousand; and there was a desperate need for a church in the northwest corner of the expanding city. It would not be an easy place for ministry, for there was a great deal of poverty and vice, and the minister would have over four thousand souls in his parish. "A city given to idolatry and hardness of heart," was the way the youthful preacher described Dundee. But then he added, "Perhaps the Lord will make this wilderness of chimney-tops to be green and beautiful as the garden of the Lord, a field which the Lord hath blessed!"

The church called McCheyne to be their pastor, and he was ordained and installed on November 24, 1836. He would minister at St. Peter's less than seven years; for he preached his last sermon there March 12, 1843, and was called Home on March 25. But in those few years, he made an impact on Scotland that is still felt, and that spiritual impact has continued over the years and has spread throughout the church. The reason that McCheyne's life and ministry continue to enrich us is because he was a man of God.

To begin with, McCheyne was careful and consistent in his devotional life. It was his happy custom to spend time before breakfast reading the Scriptures (three chapters a day), singing hymns (he was an excellent musician), and praying. He followed the counsel of that godly seventeenth-century Anglican, Jeremy Taylor; "If thou meanest to enlarge thy religion, do it rather by enlarging thine ordinary devotions than thy extraordinary." This is good counsel for today. Far too many Christians are scurrying around looking for special meetings, thinking that extraordinary experiences will make them better Christians. In my own ministry in pastors' conferences, I have discovered that too many ministers neglect their daily devotional time, or hurry through it, so they can get involved in "more important matters."

Another factor was McCheyne's sincere burden for souls. He wrote to his friend, Rev. W. C. Burns: "I feel there are two things it is impossible to desire with sufficient ardour—personal holiness, and the honour of Christ in the salvation of souls." Early in his ministry, in 1834, when he heard that a sinner had turned to Christ through hearing him preach, McCheyne wrote in his journal: "The precious tidings that a soul has been melted down by the grace of the Saviour . . . Lord, I thank Thee that Thou hast shown me this marvellous working, though I was but an adoring spectator rather than an instrument.

When McCheyne preached, it was out of a full heart of love for his people. He lamented in his journal: "In the morning was more engaged in preparing the head than the heart." When his friend Bonar told McCheyne that his text the previous Sunday had been, "The wicked shall be turned into hell,"

McCheyne asked, "Were you able to preach it with *tenderness?*"
He used to pray, "Give me Thy gentle Spirit, that neither strives
nor cries."

He prepared his messages carefully and was a diligent student. "Beaten oil," he used to say, "beaten oil for the lamps of
the sanctuary" (referring to Exod. 27:20). He brought into the
pulpit fresh manna that he had gathered himself in his personal fellowship with the Lord. No borrowed sermons, no last-
minute concoctions. His sermons were considered long, but
they are full of spiritual nutrition. He wrote to a friend, "I
cannot say that my sermons are much shorter, though I have
tried to shorten them." He received many invitations to preach
and had a difficult time refusing. In one of the last letters he
wrote, he said, "I preached twenty-seven times when I was
away, in twenty-four different places."

McCheyne drew spiritual help from the great saints of the
past. In his journal and letters, you find him mentioning such
classics as *The Letters of Samuel Rutherford* (another saintly Scot);
The Memoirs of Henry Martyn; The Christian Ministry by Charles
Bridges; *The Life and Journal of David Brainerd;* Richard Bax-
ter's *Call to the Unconverted;* and *The Works of Jonathan Edwards.* How much richer we would be if we would refuse the
books of the hour and discover again the books of the ages.

Because of his saintly life and Spirit-anointed ministry,
McCheyne was envied by some ministers, criticized by others;
but he maintained a loving attitude toward all. In fact, he
rejoiced at the blessings God gave to his brethren in the ministry. While McCheyne was on a missionary tour for the Church
of Scotland in 1839, revival broke out in his church under the
ministry of Rev. William C. Burns. On hearing the good news,
McCheyne wrote to Burns: "You remember it was the prayer
of my heart when we parted, that you might be a thousandfold
more blessed to the people than ever my ministry had been."

During a period of illness, he asked several ministers of different denominations to take his place, and for this he was
publicly criticized. He published an open letter in the *Dundee
Warder*, in which he stated that "all who are true servants of

the Lord Jesus Christ, sound in the faith, called to the ministry, and owned of God therein, should love one another, pray one for another, bid one another God-speed, own one another as fellow-soldiers, fellow-servants, and fellow-laborers in the vineyard; and, so far as God offereth opportunity, help one another in the work of the ministry." He was a man with a large heart and a great love for the people of God.

McCheyne had never been a strong man, and he overtaxed himself in his work. Once he fainted in the pulpit, and often he had to lie still for hours to encourage his palpitating heart to quiet down. He became ill at a church meeting on March 13, 1843, and had to be put to bed and given constant medical attention. He became delirious on the twenty-first, but even then was repeatedly praying or quoting Scripture. On Saturday morning the twenty-fifth, while his doctor was standing by, McCheyne lifted his hand as if to give a benediction, and then stepped into eternity.

"Live so as to be missed!" was one of his favorite sayings. Between six and seven thousand people assembled for the funeral procession; business was almost at a standstill in Glasgow. He was buried next to St. Peter's Church, and you can visit his grave today. I recall standing there one quiet June evening, reading the inscription on the monument. Then we were ushered into the vestry where the church officer opened a closet and brought out McCheyne's own Bible. I am not given to sentiment, but I must confess that I was deeply moved as I turned the pages of the Bible and read McCheyne's own annotations in the margins. It was a high and holy hour I cannot forget.

He was only thirty years old when he died, and he had ministered less than seven years at St. Peter's Church; yet his ministry and influence go on (it is interesting that two of his models in the ministry also died young: David Brainerd, at thirty; and Henry Martyn, at thirty-two). *The Memoirs and Remains of Robert Murray McCheyne*, by his dear friend Andrew Bonar, is a Christian classic that should be in every believer's library. Get the complete Banner of Truth edition, not a condensed version, and do not speed-read the book; read it carefully and meditate on what you read. I have often turned to McCheyne in dry, disappointing hours and have never failed to find refreshment for my soul.

"To gain entire likeness to Christ," he wrote, "I ought to get a high esteem of the happiness of it. I am persuaded that God's happiness is inseperably linked in with His holiness."

May our happiness be in his holiness and in a growing likeness to Jesus Christ.

4

Fanny Crosby—Blind to See God

"I believe myself still really in the prime of life!" wrote Frances Jane Crosby at the age of eighty-three. She lived twelve more years, and when she died on February 12, 1915, the news flashed around the world that America's beloved composer of gospel songs, Fanny Crosby, was home with her Lord and at last could see.

Donald P. Hustad, a recognized authority on hymnology, has called Fanny Crosby "the most prolific and significant writer of gospel songs in American history." She wrote more than eight thousand songs, most of which are now forgotten. But many continue to minister to God's people: "To God Be the Glory," "Blessed Assurance," "Praise Him! Praise Him!" "Redeemed," "Jesus, Keep Me Near the Cross," "Rescue the Perishing," "All the Way My Savior Leads Me," and others. The Hope Publishing Company has hundreds of Fanny Crosby's poems in their files just waiting to be set to music.

She was born in Putnam County, New York, on March 24, 1820. when she was only six week sold she developed a minor eye inflammation, and the doctor's careless treatment left her blind. "It seemed intended by the blessed Providence of God that I should be blind all my life," she wrote in her delightful autobiography *Fanny Crosby's Life Story* (1903), "and I thank Him for the dispensation." The doctor who destroyed her sight never forgave himself and moved from the area, but Fanny Crosby held no ill will toward him. "If I could meet him now," she wrote, "I would say 'Thank you, thank you'—over and over again—for making me blind."

In fact, she claimed that if she could have her sight restored, she would not attempt it. She felt that her blindness was God's gift to her so that she could write songs for his glory. "I could not have written thousands of hymns," she said, "if I had been hindered by the distractions of seeing all the interesting and beautiful objects that would have been presented to my notice."

She wrote her first poem when she was eight years old. Here it is.

> Oh, what a happy child I am,
>   Although I cannot see!
> I am resolved that in this world
>   Contented I will be.
>
> How many blessings I enjoy
>   That other people don't!
> So weep or sigh because I'm blind,
>   I cannot, nor I won't!

Fanny was greatly influenced by her mother and grand-mother (her father died when she was very young). When the family moved to Connecticut, a neighbor, Mrs. Hawley, read to her from the Bible and taught her Bible stories. It seems unbelievable, but by the time Fanny was ten years old, she could recite the first four books of the Old Testament and the four Gospels! She could also repeat "poems almost without number." She sometimes compared her mind to a writing desk, with little compartments filled with information readily available.

It was clear that Fanny would need formal education, so on March 3, 1835, her mother took her to the famous Institution

for the Blind in New York City. She proved to be an excellent
student in everything except mathematics. In rebellion against
the subject, she wrote the following poem:

> I loathe, abhor, it makes me sick,
> To hear the word Arithmetic!

Before long, she became the resident poet for the school,
and the superintendent was concerned that the growing praise
might go to her head. So he called her into his office and gently
warned her to beware of pride. He also urged her to use her
gifts to the glory of God. "His words were bombshells," she
later admitted, "but they did me an immense amount of good."
But the real bombshell fell some months later when she was
instructed not to write any poems for three months. It was a
great trial to the young girl, because even though she did not
write them down, the poems came into her mind almost
unbidden.

Then a strange thing happened. A noted phrenologist came
to visit the school and offered to "read the bumps" on the
heads of students and faculty. He correctly identified the leading mathematical genius in the school, and when he came to
Fanny Crosby, he said, "Why, here is a poet! Give her every
advantage that she can have; let her hear the best books and
converse with the best writers; and she will make her mark in
the world." The next morning, the superintendent called Fanny
to his office and said, "You may write all the poetry you want
to."

In 1844, she published her first book of poems, and it con-
tained the first hymn she ever wrote: "An Evening Hymn." A
second volume of poems followed in 1851 and a third in 1858.
It is interesting to note that in the 1851 volume she wrote in
the preface about her declining health, yet she lived for sixty-
four more years!

Fanny Crosby's family was a great spiritual influence in her
life, and so was Hamilton Murray, one of the instructors at the
school. But it was on November 20, 1850, that Fanny Crosby

received the assurance of her salvation. She had been attending revival meetings at the Broadway Tabernacle Methodist Church in New York City, and had even gone to the altar twice. But it was during the singing of "Alas! and Did My Savior Bleed?" that God met her need. "My very soul was flooded with celestial light," she said. "For the first time I realized that I had been trying to hold the world in one hand and the Lord in the other."

Fanny Crosby was married in 1858 to Alexander Van Alstyne, who had also been a student at the school for the blind and, like Fanny, had taught there. He was a gifted musician and a perfect partner to the poetess. He died on June 18, 1902.

During the 1850s and early sixties, Fanny Crosby wrote the lyrics to many popular secular songs, some of which were even used in minstrel shows. But the turning point of her life came on February 2, 1864, when she met William Bradbury, the famous hymnwriter and publisher. "For many years, I have been wanting you to write for me," he told her. "I wish you would begin right away!" She did begin, and the result was her first gospel song, "Our Bright Home Above." Little did anyone realize that God would use her to pen over eight thousand songs in the next fifty-one years.

How did Fanny Crosby write her lyrics? "I never undertake a hymn," she explained, "without first asking the good Lord to be my inspiration in the work that I am about to do." It helped her to hold a small book in her hand, something she often did when she lectured or gave concerts. She would pray and meditate until she was in the right mood, and sometimes she would quote several hymns to herself to prime the pump. Then the ideas would come, and she would write the song in her mind and commit it to memory. At times, she would have as many as forty different songs stored away in her mind. She would let each song lie still for a few days before dictating it to a friend who would then send it off to the publisher.

Like many prolific writers, Fanny Crosby used various pseudonyms; in fact, she used more than a hundred. Some of them are Julia Stirling, Frank Gould, Carrie M. Wilson, Lyman

Cuyler, Victoria Stewart, Maud Marion, and Ella Dale. D. L. Moody's associate, Major Daniel Whittle, wrote many hymns under the pseudonym "El Nathan," so this was not an uncommon practice.

We are shocked to learn that Fanny Crosby was paid an average of two dollars for each of her poems, although in later years it was increased to ten dollars (of course, a dollar went farther back in those days). But she certainly earned eternal rewards through her ministry of song, and we today are the richer for her faithfulness.

Fanny Crosby was just a few weeks away from her ninety-fifth birthday when she was called Home, a hope she had often written about in her songs. For the first time, she could see and, best of all, she could see her Savior. Have you ever noticed how often she wrote about seeing in her lyrics? Watch for these references the next time you sing a Fanny Crosby song. Perhaps the best known of all is the chorus of "Saved by Grace."

> And I shall see Him face to face,
> And tell the story—Saved by grace.

Fanny Crosby's Life Story has been long out of print (I found my copy in an old barn in Rumney, NH), but you can secure two recent books to help you get better acquainted with this charming lady. *Fanny Crosby Speaks Again,* edited by Donald P. Hustad, is a collection of 120 previously unpublished poems by Fanny Crosby. The brief foreword and the pictures enhance the volume. It is published by Hope Publishing Company, Carol Stream, Illinois. The second volume is *Fanny Crosby* by Bernard Ruffin (Pilgrim Press), a careful biography of this composer whom the author calls a Protestant saint.

It was said of another blind hymnwriter, George Matheson, that God made him blind so he could see clearly in other ways and become a guide to men. This same tribute could be applied to Fanny Crosby, who triumphed over her handicap and used it to the glory of God.

5

Millionaire Missionary

One Sunday at the Chicago Avenue Church (which later
became The Moody Church), Dr. R. A. Torrey challenged believers to surrender their lives in total consecration to Jesus
Christ. Many stood to their feet, among them a seven-year-old
lad in a sailor-suit. No doubt some of the adults near him
smiled at his action, but the boy was deadly serious. In fact,
that step of dedication controlled his life until, eighteen short
years later, he died in Egypt, preparing to go to China as a
missionary.

That lad was William Whiting Borden, the subject of Mrs.
Howard Taylor's classic biography. *Borden of Yale '09*. Since
there has arisen a generation that knows not Borden, I think
it is time they got acquainted.

Borden was born November 1, 1887, with blue blood in his
veins and a silver spoon in his mouth. Both the Bordens and
the Whitings (his mother's family) came from distinguished
English families noted for character and achievement. Bordens
fought beside Duke William of Normandy at the Battle of Has-
tings. The first child born of European parents in Rhode Island
was Matthew Borden; the year was 1638. Colonel William
Whiting helped to found Hartford, Connecticut. Charles Whit-

ing married Elizabeth Bradford, a descendant of Governor William Bradford of Plymouth Colony. William Bradford Whiting had a distinguished career during the Revolutionary War.

Borden's father was prominent in Chicago. He had made his money in silver mining in Colorado, a venture that was backed by Chicago merchant Marshall Field. But it was his mother who had the stronger influence on her son, for she was a devoted Christian. The fellowship and ministry at the Chicago Avenue Church meant much to her, and she had little interest in the city's society life. The fact that her ancestors came over on the *Mayflower* mattered little to Mrs. Borden. The fact that she was a Christian going to heaven was of far greater value.

William received the standard grade-school education in Chicago, and then went to Hill School, Pottsdown, Pennsylvania, for his high school training. There was a strong Christian influence on the campus, and famous preachers often spoke in chapel. "Campbell Morgan was here," William wrote his mother in 1903, "and preached a fine sermon in the morning, which was said to be the best ever given here. . . . Some of the fellows thought it was a little long, but I did not and wanted more."

The fact that William was the son of a millionaire did not interfere with his normal activities as a boy. He never tried to impress anyone; he was active in student sporting events, and he kept careful accounts of his money. He even sent his mother a monthly report of his spending. He served as chairman of the Mission Study Band, and he listened carefully whenever Dr. Robert Speer, missionary statesman, came to speak to the students. William never forgot that act of consecration that he made when he was seven years old.

He graduated from Hill School in 1904, fourth in a class of forty-eight boys. He was only sixteen years old, endowed with unusual physical and mental ability, and too young to start university. It was decided that he should take a trip around the world. His traveling companion was Walter Erdman, a graduate of Princeton University and Seminary. They sailed from San Francisco on September 20, 1904, on the *S.S. Korea.* A number of missionary couples were on board, and William said that meeting them influenced him. In fact, the entire trip only strengthened his determination to be a missionary. "When I look ahead a few years," he wrote his parents, "it seems as though the only thing to do is to prepare for the foreign field."

William was moved by what he saw in Japan and China, and he was impressed by the work of the China Inland Mission. The sights in India stirred his heart, particularly the sacred city of Benares on the Ganges. A few years later, when a friend told William that he was "throwing his life away as a missionary," William calmly replied, "*You* have never seen heathenism."

But the trip involved more than sightseeing. "Walt and I have Bible study together every day when possible," William wrote to his mother, "and I enjoy it very much. . . . I pray every day for all my dear family. I also pray that God will take my life into His hands and use it for the furtherance of His kingdom as He sees best." Then he added this significant sentence: "I have so much of everything in this life, and there are so many millions who have nothing and live in darkness!"

Back home in Chicago, Mrs. Borden shared with her husband William's desire to be a missionary. I get the impression that Mr. Borden was not as spiritually minded as his wife, and no doubt his son's decision greatly disturbed him. Had William Whiting Borden devoted his life to business interests, there is little question that he would have become a multimillionaire. But, a missionary? That was quite something else!

"I am glad that you have told Father about my desire to be a missionary," William confided in his mother, writing from Rome. "I am thinking about it all the time, and looking forward to it with a good deal of anticipation. I know that I am not at all fitted or prepared yet, but in the next four or five years I ought to be able to prepare myself." A book on missions by Robert Speer especially touched him. "When I got through reading," he wrote his mother, "I knelt right down and prayed

more earnestly than I have for some time for the mission work
and for God's plan for my life. . . . Pray that I may be guided
in everything, small and great!"

Dr. Torrey was preaching in London when William and Walt
arrived there, and they attended some of the meetings. At the
close of one of the meetings, William stood again to reaffirm
the commitment he had made to Christ more than ten years
before. This new step of dedication seemed to give him a greater
burden for the lost and a new freedom in personal witness.

William would have preferred to attend the Moody Bible
Institute and then go to college, but his parents decided he
should go to Yale University instead. He entered the freshman
class in 1905 and discovered that, in spite of the school's historic Christian background, there was a lack of spiritual life
on campus. "The great majority [of students] smoke, go to the
theatre Saturday night and do their studying on Sunday," he
wrote home. "Rather a hopeless state of affairs! However, there
are some fine Christian men in College and in my own class
too, I believe. And I hope to be able to do something, by the
grace of God, to help in the right direction."

And he did. He refused to join any secret societies or frater-
nities, and he chose friends whose spiritual interests were akin
to his own. He boldly witnessed for Christ and backed up that
witness with such a consistent life that even the unbelievers
had to admit he was a Christian. He chose two texts as his
mottos for his college years: "Wherewithal shall a young man
cleanse his way? By taking heed thereto according to thy
word. . . . Thy word have I hid in mine heart that I might not
sin against thee" (Ps. 119:9, 11).

William became burdened for the indigent people in the
seaport town of New Haven where Yale was located. The result
was the founding of the Yale Hope Mission, where William
often went to witness for Christ and to help those whose lives
had been battered by sin. "What has impressed you most since
you came to America?" Dr. Henry Frost, China Inland Mission
executive, asked a visitor. The reply: "The sight of that young
millionaire kneeling with his arm around a 'bum' in the Yale

Hope Mission." Hundreds of lives were dramatically changed through the gospel witness at the mission.

While at Yale, William served as a delegate to the Student Volunteer Movement conference at Nashville, Tennessee. The one speaker who stood out to the young missionary candidate was Dr. Samuel Zwemer, noted missionary to the Muslims. When William learned that there were 15 million Muslims in China, without a single missionary, his interest was aroused; and he commited himself to that ministry "should the Lord confirm the call." Four years later, as a delegate to the historic Edinburgh Missionary Conference, when he was introduced. Borden stated publicly that he planned to minister to the Muslims of North-West China.

He graduated from Yale in 1909 and that same year entered Princeton Seminary. He was also named a trustee of the Moody Bible Institute. The next year, he became a member of the North American Council of the China Inland Mission. William's father had died in 1906, and his mother moved to Princeton, N.J., to be near her son during those important years of preparation. Two interesting facts should be noted about his seminary years: he taught a Sunday school class in an African Methodist Episcopal Church, and he gave away $70,000 to various Christian causes.

The story now draws to a rapid close. He graduated from seminary in 1912 and, on September 9, was ordained at The Moody Church in Chicago. Dr. James M. Gray preached the ordination sermon, and Dr. John Timothy Stone, pastor of Chicago's Fourth Presbyterian Church, gave the charge to the candidate. The newspapers gave great publicity to the event, so strange it was that a young millionaire would bury himself in China as a missionary. William wrote to his school friends: "I am sorry that there was such unnecessary publicity, and hope you fellows will discount what was said very liberally."

Borden spent the next three months speaking in various colleges, representing the cause of world missions. On December 17, 1912, he sailed for Egypt where he planned to study with Dr. Zwemer and get a grasp of the Muslim religion and

culture. He threw himself into literature distribution and
whatever ministry would help to reach the lost. But just at
Easter season, 1913, he became ill with cerebral meningitis;
and died on April 9. The news of his death was reported around
the world, with memorial services held in many schools and
churches. In his will, Borden left his fortune to various Christian ministries. In his life and death he left to all of us an
example of true devotion to Christ and to the things that matter most.

Why should such a gifted life be cut short? Perhaps the best
answer was given by Sherwood Day, one of Borden's missionary friends. "I have absolutely no feeling of a life cut short,"
Day wrote. "A life abandoned to Christ cannot be cut short."
From many parts of the world, Mrs. Borden received letters
telling of the impact of her son's life and death on Christian
students and missionaries. Dr. Zwemer, in the funeral message, summarized the meaning of Borden's testimony: "By
some, the victory has to be won over poverty . . . but Borden
won the victory over an environment of wealth. He felt that
life consisted not in 'the abundance of things that a man pos-
sesseth,' but in the abundance of things which possess the
man."

After all, it is not the length of a person's life that matters,
but the strength of one's influence for God. A Judas would read
Borden's life and sneer, "Why this waste!" but our Lord would
evaluate it differently. William Whiting Borden never got to
minister to the Muslims in China, but God knew the intent of
his heart and rewarded him accordingly. Borden's desire was
to magnify Christ "whether it be by life, or by death," and God
gave him his desire.

One lesson is clear: never underestimate the decisions made
by a child or a young man. At the age of seven, Borden consecrated himself to Christ. When a freshman at Yale, he wrote
in his notebook: "Lord Jesus, I take hands off, as far as my life
is concerned. I put Thee on the throne in my heart. Change,
cleanse, use me as Thou shalt choose. I take the full power of

Thy Holy Spirit. I thank Thee." Then he added this revealing sentence: "May never know a tithe of the result until Morning."

The words of martyred Jim Elliot come to mind: "He is no fool to give what he cannot keep, to gain what he cannot lose."

And the words of our Savior: "He that loveth his life shall lose it; and he that hateth his life in this world shall keep it unto life eternal" (John 12:25).

6

Fanny Crosby's British Counterpart

Frances Ridley Havergal was to Great Britain what Fanny Crosby was to the United States, and the two women had a great deal in common. Both had to put up with physical limitations: Crosby was blind, and Havergal endured what the Victorians called delicate health, including a great deal of pain, all her life. Each of them was converted early in life and then had a deeper life experience in later years. Both were gifted singers and instrumentalists as well as gifted writers, and both had phenomenal memories.

Though they never met on earth, the two Franceses corresponded and loved one another across the miles. Havergal sent Fanny Crosby a long poem, "An English Tribute to Fanny Crosby," which ends:

> Dear blind sister over the sea.
> An English heart goes forth to thee!
> We are linked by a cable of faith and song,
> Flashing bright sympathy swift along;
> One in the east and one in the west,
> Singing for Him whom our souls love best;

"Singing for Jesus," telling His love,
All the way to our home above,
Where the severing sea, with its restless tide,
Never shall hinder, and never divide.
Sister, what will our meeting be,
When our hearts shall sing and our eyes shall see!

While Fanny Crosby excelled in writing the gospel songs. Frances Ridley Havergal's songs were more of a devotional nature, calling believers to a deeper dedication to Christ. Her most famous dedication hymn is "Take My Life and Let It Be," which she wrote on February 4, 1874, after a thrilling night of praise and prayer because of a very special victory the Lord had given her.

But we are also familiar with "Lord, Speak to Me that I May Speak," "Like a River Glorious," "Who Is on the Lord's Side?" and "I Gave My Life for Thee."

Frances Ridley Havergal was born December 14, 1836, in Astley, Worcestershire, England, where her father, William Henry Havergal, was vicar of the Astley Anglican church. She inherited her musical ability from her father, who was quite well known as a writer and publisher of church music. She learned to read by the time she was three, and when she was four, she was reading the Bible.

She discovered her talent for writing verses when she was seven and kept a notebook of what most people would call childish rhymes. But those rhymes prepared the way for her prolific writing ministry in later years. Her mother often said to her, "Fanny dear, pray to God to prepare you for all that He is preparing for you." Frances even wrote long letters in rhyme to her brother Frank and to some of her young friends. One of her little poems proved to be prophetic.

Sunday is a pleasant day,
    When we to church do go;
For there we sing and read and pray,
    And hear the sermon too.
And if we love to pray and read

> While we are in our youth,
> The Lord will help us in our need
> And keep us in His truth.

Her mother died when Frances was only eleven years old. On that day, July 5, 1848, Frances wrote in her notebook:

> Eye hath not seen, nor ear hath heard,
> Neither can man's heart conceive,
> The blessed things God hath prepared
> For those who love Him and believe.

God had been working in her heart, and she desperately wanted to know for sure that she was converted and going to heaven. The struggle lasted more than three years. A sermon she heard on divine judgment "haunted" her, and each time she witnessed the Lord's Supper, she was deeply moved. But it was while she was away at school in 1851 that she found the peace of salvation. God used the witness of a newly converted friend and the counsel of Miss Caroline Cook, who later became her stepmother, to bring her assurances of eternal life.

Frances spent a year in Germany and there received professional confirmation that she did indeed have musical and poetic gifts of the highest quality. A remarkable student, she was competent not only in music and writing, but also in languages: she knew Greek, Hebrew, Latin, German, French, and Italian. According to her sister Maria, Frances had memorized all of the Gospels and Epistles, as well as Isaiah (her favorite book), the Psalms, the Minor Prophets, and the Revelation!

In 1858 she returned to Germany with her father, who was seeking further treatment for his afflicted eyes; and it was then that she wrote "I Gave My Life for Thee." Visiting a pastor's home, she saw a picture of the crucifixion on the wall, and under it the motto, "I did this for thee. What hast thou done for me?" Quickly she took a pencil and wrote the words that are so familiar to Christians everywhere; but she was dissatisfied with them, so she threw the paper in the fire. *The paper immediately came out unharmed!* She kept the poem and later showed it to her father, who not only encouraged her to keep it but also wrote a tune for it. However, the tune we usually use today was written by Philip P. Bliss.

As Frances matured, she found herself being used of God in writing, teaching the Bible, visiting the poor and afflicted, and corresponding with people who felt led to share their problems with her. She taught a children's Sunday school class at whatever church her father was pastoring, and she kept a permanent register of their names so that she might pray for them. I wonder what would happen to our children and young people if each teacher who had ministered to them continued to pray for them?

In 1865, Frances was very ill at a time when many opportunities were open to her. "I am held back from much I wanted to do in every way, and have had to lay poetizing aside," she wrote in 1866. "And yet such open doors seemed set before me. Perhaps this check is sent that I may consecrate what I do more entirely. . . . I suppose that God's crosses are often made of most unexpected and strange material."

In 1869, her first book, *Ministry of Song*, was published. A decade earlier her doctor had told her that she must choose between writing and living because her health would not permit her to do both. "Did you ever hear of any one being very much used for Christ who did not have some special waiting time, some complete upset of all his or her plans?" she wrote. When *Ministry of Song* was published, Frances testified that she saw "the evident wisdom of having been kept nine years waiting in the shade."

There were other tests besides her recurring illnesses and almost constant weakness. In 1874, her American publisher went bankrupt in the economic crash; and since she had an exclusive contract with him, this put an end to her American publishing until the business could get back on its feet again. This meant, of course, a loss of income as well.

"Two months ago, this would have been a real trial to me," she wrote to a friend, "for I had built a good deal on my American prospects; now, 'Thy will be done' is not a sigh but only *a song!* . . . I have not a fear, or a doubt, or a care, or a shadow upon the sunshine of my heart."

The secret of her victory is found in an experience she had on December 2, 1873, just two months before she received news of the crash. A friend had mailed her a copy of a little booklet entitled *All for Jesus*. It kindled in her heart a deep desire for greater consecration and wider usefulness, and she began to pray to that end. God answered her prayers. She wrote:

"Yes, it was on Advent Sunday, December 2nd, 1873, I first saw clearly the blessedness of true consecration. I saw it as a flash of electric light. . . . There must be full surrender before there can be full blessedness." She discovered the meaning of I John 1:7 and the importance of trusting Christ *to keep her* as well as to save her. She totally rejected all ideas of "sinless perfection," but claimed the clear biblical teaching of constant victory. "Not a coming to be cleansed in the fountain only," she explained, "but a *remaining* in the fountain, so that it may and can go on cleansing." Her knowledge of Greek told her that the verb in I John 1:9 is present—"keeps on cleansing." The next time you sing "Like a River Glorious," keep in mind that it is Frances Ridley Havergal's testimony to the reality of the victorious Christian life.

Francis never sat down with the determination to write a poem or a song. "Writing is *praying* with me," she said, "for I never seem to write even a verse by myself, and feel like a little child writing; you know a child would look up at every sentence and say, 'And what shall I say next?' That is just what I do." It was her conviction that God had a message for her to share and that he would direct her in the writing of it. If nothing came to her, she accepted the silence and went on to other things. "The Master has not put a chest of poetic gold into my possession and said, 'Now use it as you like!' " she wrote to a friend. "But He keeps the gold, and gives it to me piece by piece just when He will and as much as He will, and no more." Sometimes that gold included chords and melodies as well, for Frances was an accomplished musician.

In 1876, Frances went through another fiery trial: the offices of her British publisher burned down, and with it went the complete manuscript and plates of *Songs of Grace and Glory*, which she had recently completed. She had not kept a copy of much of this material, so she had to begin all over again, not only with the words but also the music. "I have thanked Him for it," she wrote to her sisters, "more than I have prayed about it. It is just what He did with me last year, it is another *turned lesson*." God gave her sufficient health and strength to do the work again.

Her daily quiet time with the Lord was kept with loving discipline, and she always devoted extra time to serious Bible study. (One wishes that some of our contemporary composers would spend more time in their Bibles and put more solid theology into their songs.) Hymn writing was not a business with Frances; it was a ministry. Even her singing and playing in public were not considered performances but opportunities for her to glorify Christ and share him with others. She had a very sane and scriptural view of true consecration.

"Consecration is not so much a step as a course," she wrote in her devotional classic *Kept for the Master's Use*, "not so much an act as a position to which a course of action inseparably belongs. . . . Does this mean that we are always to be doing some definitely religious work, as it is called? No, but all that we do is to be always definitely done for Him." There was a time in her life when she decided she would not sing or play secular songs, although she did not criticize those who did so. She could have become a famous concert artist had she pursued such a career, but to her, it was not consistent with her Christian witness. She made this decision several months before she wrote:

> Take my lips, and let me sing,
> Always, only, for my King.

During 1873, on a visit to Switzerland, she was almost killed in a climbing accident; and in 1874 she suffered for eight months with typhoid fever. But she continued to write, as the Lord enabled her, and she carried on a wide correspondence. In one six-month period, she received over six hundred letters.

Her last year of ministry on earth was 1879. She kept a "Journal of Mercies," and some of the entries are interesting when you consider her weakened condition. "Able to come downstairs for the first time," she wrote on New Year's Day. On January 14, she wrote, "Being withheld from resuming work, and sense of God's wise hand in it." "Strength for extra pulls" was the entry for February 5, and on February 23 she wrote, "Freedom from pain."

During those difficult days, she also kept a prayer list with daily needs and special requests for each day. She also made a list of "work for 1879, if the Lord wills." On that list was her desire to prepare for the press *Kept for the Master's Use;* and God granted her that desire. She finished revising the proofs shortly before her death on June 3, 1879. At the time, she was living at Caswall Bay in Wales, near Swansea; but the family took her body back to Astley where she was buried on June 9 beside other family members in the beloved churchyard of her childhood days.

The next year, her sister Maria published *Memorials of Frances Ridley Havergal* (London: James Nisbet), a book that is now long out of print. Baker Book House has reprinted *Kept for the Master's Use* and *Royal Bounty,* two of her finest devotional books. Both books reveal her love for Scripture and her ability to understand and teach it. She was far more than a musician and poetess. She was a unique woman with a penetrating ministry that was fashioned in the furnace of suffering.

When her doctor said to her, "Goodbye, I shall not see you again," Frances asked, "Then do you really think I am going?" He replied, "Yes."

"Today?" she asked, and he said, "Probably."

Her response was. "Beautiful—too good to be true!" But that would be the response of any believer who had honestly said.

> Take my life, and let it be,
> Consecrated, Lord, to Thee!

7

Bonar—Minister with the Laughing Face

One of the richest experiences you can have is reading the diaries and journals of great men and women in Christian history. Among many that I enjoy, perhaps my favorite is *The Diary and Life of Andrew Bonar*, edited by his daughter, Marjory Bonar, and published by Banner of Truth Trust.

Most people know Andrew Bonar as the brother of hymn-writer Horatius Bonar, and the close friend of Robert Murray McCheyne. He was also the editor of the best edition of Samuel Rutherford's *Letters*, and the author of a devotional commentary on Leviticus and *Christ and His Church in the Book of Psalms*, which has been reprinted by Kregel Publications.

But when you read his journal, you will meet and learn to love a truly great man of God. He lived and labored at a critical time in the church in Scotland, and God used him in wonderful ways to uphold his truth and build his people.

Andrew Alexander Bonar was born on May 29, 1810, in Edinburgh, Scotland, the seventh son of James and Marjory Bonar. He was surrounded by spiritual influences, but not until he was twenty years old and in college did he have assurance of his salvation.

Later, he became a divinity student, and during that time cultivated his friendship with McCheyne. He served as an assistant pastor and city missionary in Jedburgh and at St. George's in Edinburgh, and was licensed in 1824. In 1836, he candidated at St. Peter's Church, Dundee, but the congregation called McCheyne instead.

In 1838 Bonar accepted a call to the Presbyterian Church in Collace, where he was ordained and remained for eighteen fruitful years. When he arrived, there were probably only half a dozen true believers in the parish; but God sent revival to the area, and many turned to Christ. While Bonar and McCheyne were on a special missionary deputation to the Holy Land in 1839, God used William Burns to bring a fresh wind of the Spirit to McCheyne's church in Dundee, and the blessing spread to other churches.

The year 1843 was difficult for ministers and churches in Scotland, for in that year more than four hundred dedicated ministers left the Established Church and founded the Free Church. Those who seceded protested the modernistic tendencies of the denomination and the interference of the civil courts in church affairs. At Collace, Bonar preached in a tent until the congregation, which had forfeited its property, could build a new place of worship.

In 1856, Bonar became pastor of a new church on Finnieston Street in a needy area of Glasgow; and there he remained until his death on December 30, 1892. Before long what had been a small work when he began had grown to a congregation of more than a thousand members, with a strong Sunday school program and an evangelistic outreach into the city. The work was difficult, but Bonar preached the Word and trusted God. When a friend asked one day how things were going, Bonar replied, "Oh, we are looking for great things!" When his friend admonished him not to expect too much, Bonar replied, "We can never hope for too much!"

A confirmed premillennialist, Bonar enjoyed preaching about the return of Jesus Christ. He had a remarkable ability to remember names and faces. One day he addressed by name a little girl on the street, and she ran home and announced, "Mother, Mother, he knows me!"

He could detect when a member was absent on Sunday and during the week would visit to see if there were a special problem or need. He also had a marvelous sense of humor. One child called him "the minister with the laughing face." One day he told an invalid he was visiting, "I have a new medicine for you: 'A merry heart doeth good like a medicine.'" When a man told Bonar he had felt an angel touch him during an illness, Bonar said, "Have you a cat in the house? Don't you think it may have been the cat?"

He believed in pastoral work, particularly visiting in people's homes. "There is a blessing resting on visiting," he wrote to a pastor friend. "What else is fitted to make us know the state of our flocks? Were it not for their good but only for our own, is not this department of work most important? It is only thus we can know our people's spiritual state." He usually visited every afternoon from one o'clock to five, walking great distances to bring encouragement and help to his beloved people.

I think the greatest value of the *Diary and Life* is its record of Bonar's interior life. He was able to accomplish much with men in public because he spent time with God in private. There are scores of references in these pages to prayer, meditation, and self-examination. They also record times of discouragement and defeat when Bonar felt he had failed the Lord and his people. God's choicest servants rarely evaluate their own ministries with accuracy and balance, and often Bonar was too hard on himself.

During the Kilsyth Revival of 1839–40, Bonar wrote to his brother Horace: "Pray for Collace. We have no more than a few drops as yet, and I believe I am to blame. I *work* more than I *pray*." Later he wrote in his journal: "I was living very grossly, namely, laboring night and day in visiting with very little prayerfulness. I did not see that prayer should be the main business of every day." Again, he wrote: "I see that prayerlessness is one of my great sins of omission. I am too short, ask too little, ask with too much want of forethought. Then, *too little meditation upon Scripture."*

He discovered that even his books and his literary ministry could create problems in his spiritual life. "Tried this morning specially to pray against idols in the shape of my books and studies. These encroach upon my direct communion with God, and need to be watched." As he was writing *Christ and His Church in the Book of Psalms,* he noted in his diary: "I distinctly see now that Satan's chief way of prevailing against me is by throwing in my way a great deal of half literary work, half biblical." When he was preparing *Rutherford's Letters,* he wrote: "A piece of extra work this year has been an edition of *Rutherford's Letters,* which I fear has been a snare to me, inasmuch as it has sometimes shortened prayer, yet it has also helped me."

Bonar tried to keep each Saturday evening as a time of prayer and special preparation of his own soul for the ministry on the Lord's Day, a practice I strongly recommend to preachers today. But he discovered that he was especially vulnerable to Satan's attacks on Saturday evenings and Monday mornings. He often sought for "Saturday assurances" from God to encourage him for his Sunday ministry. He observed that Christ, after a busy day of ministry, arose early to pray (Mark 1:35); and he tried to follow that example on Monday mornings.

In spite of his success as a pastor, preacher, and writer, Bonar often saw himself as a failure in the pulpit. On December 5, 1857, he wrote in his diary: "Got such a sight of the impotence of my preaching that I felt as if I need never attempt it more." One day he received special encouragement from Proverbs 23:16, "Yea, my reins shall rejoice, when thy lips speak right things." He wrote in his journal, "Christ listening to our sermons!"

Bonar realized that he could not go on forever, no matter how much his people loved him. There is a deeply touching entry in his diary for September 11, 1890, when he was eighty years old.

I see distinctly that my Lord is teaching me to "glory in my
infirmities" and to be willing to be set aside. My voice fails;
some of my people, specially the younger part, going elsewhere;
my class melts away. Some very mortifying cases of ingrati-
tudes on the part of some; my influence with brethren mani-
festly declines—all this is saying, "He must increase, but I must
decrease."

On October 14, a committee met with him to arrange to call
a successor. "I read with them Numbers 27:15–18, and prayed
with thanksgiving, and the business went on pleasantly," he
wrote.

"Oh, I don't think anything about growing old," Bonar once
told D. L. Moody's associate, Major D. W. Whittle. But those
closest to him detected a gradual failing of his strength, even
though he continued in ministry as much as possible; and after
only two days of illness, he went Home to Glory on Friday,
December 30, 1892.

Each time I read Bonar's *Diary and Life*, I find something
new to ponder, or I am reminded of something I had already
read and underlined, but had forgotten. His personal character
has always impressed me. He was not envious at the success
of others, but rejoiced at God's blessing, even if he disagreed
with the methods other men used.When many Calvinists were
opposing Moody and Sankey, Bonar was praying for them and
laboring with them. Moody invited him to minister at this
Northfield Conference, and in 1881 Bonar sailed to America
and ministered in several cities. Like F. B. Meyer, Henry Drum-
mond, and many other ministers of the Word, Bonar was greatly
helped by his friendship with Moody.

I have also been impressed with Bonar's emphasis on evangelism. He kept two texts (in the original Hebrew) in his study:
"He that winneth souls is wise" (Prov. 11:30) and "For yet a
little while, and He that shall come will come and will not
tarry" (Hab. 2:3). When the church in Finnieston Street moved
to a new location in 1878, "He that winneth souls is wise" was
carved in Hebrew over the front door. Bonar had a special
burden for the Jews, and he hoped that the text would not

only attract them but also remind his own people of the importance of witnessing.

Although Bonar was criticized by some and ignored by others, he stuck to his premillennial interpretation of the Word and greatly advanced the study of prophecy in Great Britain. He viewed the Lord's return as a practical motivation for life and ministry. His views closed doors for him, but they also opened many hearts.

Bonar noted in his diary on July 5, 1847: "I have been much impressed with the sin of choosing my text without special direction from the Lord. This is like running without being sent, no message being given me." He also tried to relate each text to the needs of his people. "I feel as if I had not got my subject from the Lord," he wrote in 1858. "This whole matter had led me to search into my feelings toward my people, and I have discovered that I do not sufficiently think of them individually and pray for them . . . Lord, give me a larger heart and a holier to me."

In my own preaching ministry, I have quoted some of Andrew Bonar's "spiritual sayings," and I want to close with some of my favorites.

The best part of all Christian work is that part which only God sees.

If the Father has the kingdom ready for us, He will take care of us on the way.

Lot would not give up Christ, but he would not give up much *for* Christ.

Let us be as watchful after the victory as before the battle.

God likes to see His people shut up to this, that there is no hope but in prayer. Herein lies the Church's power against the world.

Love is the *motive* for working; joy is the *strength* for working.

We have got more from Paul's prison-house than from his visit to the third heaven.

He had a card in his study near the mantelpiece that read: "He who has truly prayed has completed the half of his study."

"The sins of teachers are the teachers of sins."

"Beware of the bad things of good men."

Bonar was pleased when the University of Edinburgh granted him a Doctor of Divinity degree in 1873. But when he was made Moderator of the Free Church Assembly, he said: "Alas! How far down our Church has come when it asks such as me to take this office!"

"Many want salvation, but they do not want the Saviour."

Finally, "You need not be afraid of too much grace. Great grace never makes a man proud. A little grace is very apt to make a man be puffed up."

I hope you will get acquainted with this delightful man of God—a wholesome example in ministry, and a saint who encourages us to live in the Holy of Holies with God.

8

The Preacher
Who Couldn't Preach

On August 27, 1876, a twelve-year-old boy faced a small group of people in a schoolroom and preached his first sermon. Nearly sixty-seven years to the day, on August 29, 1943, he preached his last sermon at Westminster Chapel, London, a church that became famous because of his ministry. Between those two events, George Campbell Morgan had become "the prince of expositors," perhaps the greatest Bible teacher of that day in the English-speaking world.

And yet, he had no formal training in either college or seminary. He presented himself as a candidate for ministry with the Methodists, who rejected him. They said he could not preach! On that discouraging day, May 2, 1888, he sent a wire to his father, also a preacher, which said "Rejected."

His father wired back: "Rejected on earth, accepted in heaven." Indeed, heaven did bless Morgan's life and ministry, and we today are the richer for it.

He was born in the little village of Tetbury, Gloucestershire, on December 9, 1863. His parents were godly people of the old Puritan stock, and his father had resigned as pastor of a Baptist church because of certain biblical convictions that he held. He

48

was preaching the Word as he felt God wanted it preached in a rented hall in Tetbury. He passed along this courage of conscience to his son, for during his own ministry, Campbell Morgan refused to cater to the crowd at the expense of truth. More than once he was "rejected on earth, accepted in heaven."

Young Morgan was finally accepted by the Congregationalists and was ordained September 22, 1890. He pastored small churches in the villages of Stone and Rugeley from 1889 to 1893, then moved to a larger work in Birmingham. His gift for Bible teaching was soon discovered by D. L. Moody, who invited him to minister in Northfield in 1896. From 1897 to 1901, Morgan pastored New Court Church, Tollington Park, North London. He also made two visits to the United States and Canada for ministry during those years. In all, Morgan crossed the Atlantic fifty-four times during his lifetime.

Moody invited Morgan to head the extension ministry of the Northfield Bible Conference; so on June 12, 1901, the Morgans sailed for the United States and moved into a crowded schedule and a busy life. Moody had died six months before; but his son, Will Moody, took over the Northfield work and insisted that Morgan come. The great Joseph Parker of City Temple, London, called it burglary when he heard Morgan was leaving Britain. But there seemed to be no center in Britain from which Morgan could carry out his plans for teaching the Word of God to people who heard plenty of sermons but were still starved for truth.

It was Moody who "found" Morgan, and it was the Christian community in the United States that took him to heart and encouraged him in his work. It is worth noting that Moody was "found" by Britain and came back to the States after a series of successful revivals to discover he was a famous man.

However, Morgan was not to remain in the United States. The officers of Westminster Chapel, Buckingham Gate, London, sought him as their pastor. After months of waiting and praying, the church received the news on June 19, 1904, that Morgan had accepted. His ministry of the Word and his adaptation of American methods of church management soon transformed a derelict church into a powerhouse for God. Great crowds gathered to hear the Word expounded, and many came to trust Christ as a result. Morgan still kept up a demanding wider ministry during the week, and in this way encouraged thousands in their personal Bible study.

But he was not a well man. After his tenth anniversary at Westminster, he was seriously ill for three months. He often had throat problems and severe headaches. He tried to resign the church once, but the church refused to accept it. Finally, in January, 1917, he left the church and spent the next sixteen years primarily ministering in the United States. He visited Britain often and preached often at Westminster, but his home was in the States.

He lived in Athens, Georgia, for a time; then in Ohio, Indiana, California, and Pennsylvania. One of Morgan's friends called him a nomad, and perhaps he was right. But wherever he ministered the Word, great crowds gathered, listened, and went away with a new love for the Bible and a new desire to study it.

In 1933, when he was seventy years old, Morgan was called back to Westminster, and he accepted the call. He had shepherded the church through the First World War, and now he would guide them through the Second. In 1938, he added Dr. D. Martyn Lloyd-Jones as his associate minister; and in June, 1943, Morgan resigned and turned the church over to Lloyd-Jones. Morgan died May 16, 1945.

I have read Morgan's life many times and have saturated myself with his sermons and Bible expositions; and he always has something new to say to me. He published eleven volumes of sermons, *The Westminster Pulpit*, as well as ten volumes of *The Analyzed Bible*, and thirty-nine other volumes of expositions and studies. Add to these titles eleven booklets, and you have a grand total of seventy-one publications. At one stage in his life, Morgan was publishing three books a year.

What was the secret of his ministry? Of course, he was a man of God who depended on the Lord for his messages; but many godly people never seem to get much done in the place where God has called them. After studying Morgan's life and ministry, I think I have come up with several factors that helped him accomplish much to the glory of God.

To begin with, *he worked hard.* He began Bible study early in the morning and permitted no interruptions until lunch time. He disciplined himself to have a firsthand knowledge of the Bible, not a secondhand knowledge from other men. Even when he preached a message a second or third time in his conference ministry, he spent an extra hour going over the message and making it fresh to his own soul.

Second, Morgan's ministry was *centered in the Bible.* "We must regularly and devotionally study the Word," he wrote, "in order that we may discover the revelation of principles. When this is done as a habit of life, the mind will act under the power of those principles, and the conclusions arrived at will be in harmony with the intention of Christ." He wrote in 1938, "There is nothing I desire more in my dealing with the Bible, than to lead people to a personal appreciation and understanding of it." He did not preach about the Bible; he preached the Bible.

A third factor is that *he majored in the basics of the Christian faith.* "I have constant sorrow in my heart over the bitter theological controversies which characterize the hour," he wrote in 1923, "and the saddest thing is the spirit of them. . . . My work is wholly constructive, and I believe that that is the only kind that is really of value." He was severely attacked and criticized by the ultrafundamentalists for not fighting apostasy, but he kept on with the same positive ministry. He was not without strong convictions, and he voiced them; but he avoided name-calling and heresy-hunting. He said that "the Devil's master stroke is that of dividing forces that ought to stand together."

Another factor was *his largeness of heart and vision.* In this, he was greatly influenced by Moody. "Every man has his own particular gift and responsibility," he said, "and mine is far more catholic [universal] than denominational." He affirmed that he preached "positive New Testament truth . . . the central

verities of our faith." He wrote in 1913, "As I get older my
sympathies get far broader in many directions, and I thank
God for all I find of the true spirit of Christ in many places
where I never looked for it in the olden days." Because his
teaching majored on the essentials of the Christian faith and
life, he attracted listeners from many branches of the church.
The purpose of his preaching was "to declare truth," not to
promote some man-made doctrine or program.

Finally, *Morgan had the heart of an evangelist.* Many people
forget that he began his ministry as an itinerant evangelist
and was greatly used to reach the lost. At one time, he considered joining the Salvation Army because of his concern to
reach sinners. Even after he had attained eminence as a Bible
teacher and preacher, Morgan retained his burden for lost souls.
He abhorred what he called the passion for statistics, but he
never neglected to proclaim the Gospel of Christ and the Christ
of the Gospel.

To be sure, we must not rule out God's sovereignty in be-
stowing his gifts. But even though we may not become another
G. Campbell Morgan, we can still make better use of our own
gifts by learning from him. He was faithful in using his gifts,
and God blessed him. The man with one talent can get the
same reward as the man with five talents if he is faithful.

I think D. L. Moody expressed it perfectly when he said:

> A few years ago now, in England, the good Wesleyan brethren
> in that country turned him down because they were under the
> impression that he couldn't preach. Well, all I can say to that
> is, Mr. Morgan surely reaches *my* heart, and I believe him to be
> filled utterly with the Spirit of God.

A Man of the Word by Jill Morgan (Baker Book House) is the
official biography of G. Campbell Morgan, a book I try to read
again every year. *This Was His Faith;* also by his daughter-in-
law, Jill Morgan, is a collection of excerpts from his letters,
dealing with various themes. This book and *G. Campbell Morgan: The Man and His Ministry,* by John Harris, were published
by Fleming H. Revell.

9

The Apostle
of the Haphazard

"I feel I shall be buried for a time, hidden away in obscurity; then suddenly I shall flame out, do my work, and be gone."

Those words were spoken by Oswald Chambers, author of *My Utmost for His Highest* and more than thirty other books that never seem to grow old. His statement was prophetic, except that the flame God lit is still burning brightly, thanks to the printed page.

When you review the life of Oswald Chambers, you can well understand why a friend once introduced him as the apostle of the haphazard. Like the wind Jesus spoke of in John 3:8, Chambers came and went in a seeming erratic fashion; yet there was a definite plan in his life, and he was greatly used of God. He is a good reminder to boxed-in Christians that God sometimes bypasses our date-books and management-by-objectives and does the surprising, even the unexpected, in our lives.

Oswald Chambers was born in Aberdeen, Scotland, on July 24, 1874. His parents had been baptized by Charles Spurgeon, who had also ordained Chambers's father to the Baptist ministry. While the family was living in London, young Oswald, in his teens, gave his heart to Christ.

He and his father were walking home from a meeting conducted by Spurgeon, and Oswald admitted that he would have given himself to the Lord had the opportunity been given. "You can do it now, my boy!" said his father; and right there, the boy trusted Christ and was born again. He was baptized by Rev. J. T. Briscoe and became a member of the Rye Lane Baptist Church in London.

A gifted artist, Chambers entered art school in 1892 and three years later went to Edinburgh to continue his studies. In 1896, he felt a definite call to the ministry, and the following year he entered the Dunoon Training College in Scotland. Not only did he have an outstanding record as a student, but he remained after graduation to teach. He had a special interest in philosophy and psychology, and taught those courses.

But in November 1901, Chambers had a deep experience with the Lord that transformed his life. He called it a baptism of the Holy Spirit, a term I prefer to apply only to the believer's experience at conversion (see I Cor. 12:13). This special filling of the Spirit gave him new insights into both the Christian life and the courses he was then teaching. In his ministry of the Word, he reveals both the philosopher and the psychologist.

He left school in 1905 and began an itinerant ministry in Britain, the United States, and Japan. He taught at the Oriental Missionary Society Bible School in Tokyo; and then he became a "missioner" for the League of Prayer which had been founded by Reader Harris. He was married on May 25, 1910, to Gertrude Hobbs, a devoted woman who was also an expert stenographer, a fact that would mean much in the years to come.

Chambers felt there was a need for a Bible college in Britain that would emphasize personal Christian living and not just education and practical training. With the help of some friends, he founded the Bible Training College at Clapham. The school operated on faith and prayer. When a friend offered to endow the school, Chambers refused the offer saying, "No, if you do that it will probably go on longer than God means it to."

He felt led to offer himself as a military chaplain during World War I, and on October 9, 1915, he sailed with the troops for Zeitoun, Egypt, where he ministered until his untimely death on November 15, 1917. He had appendicitis and did not know it, peritonitis set in, and his life could not be saved.

At this point his wife, Gertrude, (everybody called her Biddy) and his daughter Kathleen enter the picture and become very important. Biddy remained at their home in Zeitoun and ministered for about a year. Then she and her daughter returned to England. Over the years, she had taken stenographic reports of her husband's messages and, at the request of many friends, began to edit and publish them. Oswald Chambers actually never wrote any of his books, although his name is on them. He spoke every word, but it was his wife, and later his daughter, who prepared the manuscripts and mothered each book through the presses. How grateful we are to God that Chambers married an expert stenographer!

His most famous book is *My Utmost for His Highest*, a daily devotional book that not every Christian can immediately appreciate. I recall telling a mature Christian friend many years ago that I was getting nothing out of the book. "Set it aside for a time," she counseled. "It's something you have to grow into." She was right: the problem was not the complexity of the book but the spiritual immaturity of the reader. In later years, I have come to appreciate this classic devotional book, and I learn more from it as the years go by.

Too many devotional books are finished with one reading, because they do not get down to fundamental truths that keep expanding into more truth. A good book is like seed: it produces fruit that has in it seed for more fruit. It is not a picture on the wall; it is a window that invites us to wider horizons.

Each time I read a page in *My Utmost for His Highest*, I am reminded of a forgotten nugget, or I see something new that previously had eluded me. It is a book to grow with and, as such, it is unique.

All the writings of Oswald Chambers have their value. I must confess that I get a bit tired of his alliteration, some of which seems forced; but I have learned to look beyond it. I have especially appreciated his book on Abraham, *Not Knowing Whither*. *The Philosophy of Sin* has some penetrating insights in it. Chambers was similar to F. B. Meyer in his ability to diagnose spiritual problems and give biblical solutions. *Biblical Psychology* reveals Chambers, the amateur psychologist, but the emphasis is on the Bible and not on psychology. His studies in Job, *Baffled to Fight Better*, are brief but rich, and very rewarding.

The official biography, *Oswald Chambers: His Life and Work*, was compiled and edited by his wife. She quotes from his journals, adds her own comments, and quotes from material given her by his many friends and associates in ministry. Like Chambers himself, this book is a bit haphazard, and the reader can easily lose the chronological trail. But the many quotations from Chambers, and the revelation of his personality, make its reading worthwhile. It was published in London in 1933 by Simpkin Marshall, Ltd.

What kind of a man was Oswald Chambers? For one thing, he was not a brittle and pious "saint" who lived aloof from the world and the people around him. He was very much alive, and he had a marvelous sense of humor. One man wrote to Mrs. Chambers that he had been "shocked at what I then considered his undue levity. He was the most irreverent Reverend I had ever met!"

But Chambers gave himself totally to the Lord, and this included his sense of humor. He once wrote in his journal, "Lord, keep me radiantly and joyously Thine." En route to Egypt, he conducted services on the ship and brought his humor into the messages.

"Ah, I see," said one of the men, "your jokes and lightheartedness plough the land, then you put in the seed." You could not find a better philosophy of humor in the pulpit than that.

Chambers emphasized holy living, but he did not divorce it from the practical affairs of life. "I am realizing more and more the futility of separating a life into secular and sacred. It is all His." Those words summarize his position perfectly.

He wrote to a friend, "You can be much more for Him than ever you know by just being yourself and relying on Him. . . . Keep praying and playing and being yourself." He felt that his own greatest ministry was that of intercessory prayer.

A gifted teacher, he was careful that the truths he taught were meaningful in his own life. "Views from propagandist teaching are borrowed plumes," he said "Teaching is meant to stir up thinking, not to store with goods from the outside." That is good counsel in this age when many teachers and preachers manufacture their lessons and sermons out of borrowed nuggets instead of mining their own gold and refining it in experience.

He sought to present truth in ways that would excite new interest in his listeners. One listener said, "I wondered, as I drank in his message, whether I had the same Bible as he had. The written Word became a Living Word, and as I obeyed it my whole life was altered."

He would have agreed with A. W. Tozer, that the only *real* world is the world of truth found in the Bible. He wrote: "The Actual world of things and the Real world of Truth have to be made into one in personal experience." Too many Christians try to avoid this creative tension by going either to extreme isolation from the world or to extreme preoccupation with the world.

Oswald Chambers loved books and read widely. The biography contains references to many authors of different theological positions, from Alexander Maclaren and John Henry Jowett to Emmanuel Swedenborg and Ralph Waldo Emerson. "My books!" he wrote to a friend. "I cannot tell you what they are to me—silent, wealthy, loyal lovers. . . . I do thank God for my books with every fiber of my being. Friends that are ever true and ever your own." He always integrated his wide reading with the Word of God, which he considered the only test for spiritual truth.

In many respects, Chambers was not in tune with the general spirit of evangelical Christianity in his day. On his way to Egypt, he wrote in his journal: "How unproselytizing God is!

I feel the 'soul winning campaign' is often at heart the apotheosis [glorification] of commercialism, the desire to see so much result from so much expenditure. The ordinary evangelical spirit is less and less congenial to my own soul." His writings are a good antidote to the success philosophy that has invaded the church in our own day. He said that "the 'soul saving passion' as an aim must cease and merge into the passion for Christ, revealing itself in holiness in all human relationships." In other words, soul-winning is not something we *do*, it is something we *are* twenty-four hours a day, and we live for souls because we love Christ. No counting trophies in his ministry.

He was not afraid to accept truth no matter what channel God might use to give it to him. He told students to "*soak, soak, soak* in philosophy and psychology. . . . It is ignorance of the subjects on the part of ministers and workers that has brought our evangelical theology to such a sorry plight." Both in the pulpit and classroom, and as a personal counselor, Chambers revealed his keen understanding of the Bible, the human heart and mind, and the world of thought. He was able to blend these disciplines into a total ministry that God greatly used.

Let me share a few quotations from Oswald Chambers that, I trust, will whet your appetite for more.

> You can never give another person that which you have found, but you can make him homesick for what you have.
>
> If we are saved and sanctified, God guides us by our ordinary choices, and if we are going to choose what He does not want, He will check, and we must heed.
>
> Every doctrine that is not imbedded in the Cross of Jesus will lead astray.
>
> Stop having a measuring rod for other people. There is always one fact more in every man's case about which we know nothing.
>
> It takes a long time to realize the danger of being an amateur providence, that is, interfering with God's order for others.

Our Lord's first obedience was to the will of His Father, not to the needs of men; the saving of men was the natural outcome of His obedience to the Father.

One of his sayings that is underlined in my copy of *My Utmost for His Highest* has been especially meaningful to me.

The snare in Christian work is to rejoice in successful service, to rejoice in the fact that God has used you. . . . If you make usefulness the test, then Jesus Christ was the greatest failure that ever lived. The lodestar of the saint is God Himself, not estimated usefulness. It is the work that God does through us that counts, not what we do for Him.

Mrs. Chambers died in 1966 just after she had begun to prepare the thirty-second volume for the publishers; and her daughter completed the book. How grateful to God we should be for Biddy and Kathleen for their unselfish labor of love over the years, in sharing the ministry of Oswald Chambers with us. His body is buried in the cemetery in Old Cairo, his spirit is rejoicing in the presence of God, and his ministry goes on triumphantly.

Perhaps one final quotation will sum up his philosophy of the Christian life. "Never make a principle out of your experience; let God be as original with other people as He is with you."

He may have been the apostle of the haphazard, but Oswald Chambers can assist any sincere Christian to order his life in the will of God.

10

Aristocrat in the Pulpit

The year 1759 was a good one for producing leadership in Great Britain. William Pitt the younger was born in that year and became the great political leader during the Napoleonic wars. That same year also gave Britain William Wilberforce, the Christian statesman who led the fight against slavery. But the man of that year who fascinates me the most is Charles Simeon, a neglected evangelical leader in the Anglican Church, an aristocrat who used his money and position to further the cause of the Gospel at a difficult time in church history.

He was born on September 24 into a well-to-do family in Reading, England. His father, Richard Simeon, was a wealthy lawyer, and Charles grew up accustomed to affluence. He entered Cambridge in 1779, enrolling at King's College. Extravagant in his dress, and rather handsome in features, Simeon attracted attention and took advantage of it.

Although he was not an outstanding student, classes were not particularly difficult for him, and he always managed to enjoy a good time. His first real problem arose when he discovered that, at Lenten season, he would have to join the other students in Holy Communion. Religious life at Cambridge was very low, but the traditions were carried on routinely, and the young men were expected to cooperate. "Satan himself was as fit to attend as I!" Simeon remarked in later years. He was an unconverted sinner, and he knew it.

Although he fasted and prayed and even read books on the Christian religion, the heavens were brass, and he received no light. He knew that most of the other men were also unconverted and would, like him, bluff their way through; but even this did not give him peace.

At some point early in Holy Week, Simeon ran across the statement, "The Jews knew what they did when they transferred their sin to the head of their offering." Instantly, Simeon grasped the idea of a substitute dying for his sins; and he began to have hope.

By faith, he laid his sins on Jesus Christ; but it was not until Easter Sunday morning that the full assurance of salvation gripped him. It was April 4, 1779, and he awoke with praise on his lips. He attended chapel, shared in the Communion Service, and felt a nearness to the Savior.

His conversion did not excite his family; in fact, they resisted his attempt to witness to them. He found no Christian fellowship at the university, yet he managed to keep growing and living faithfully during his student years. And his evangelical zeal made him not a few enemies. He was still an aristocrat and had much to learn about humility and service.

He was ordained a deacon of the church in 1782 and began preaching whenever he had opportunity. During the summer, he filled the pulpit at a friend's church and soon saw the building packed with attentive listeners. The zealous young man with the clear Gospel message was attracting attention. In fact, so filled was the church building that the illustrious parish clerk even lost his reserved seat. The angry clerk rejoiced when the regular pastor returned after his summer holiday, saying to him, "I am so glad you are come! Now we shall have some room!"

Simeon was appointed as minister of Holy Trinity Church, Cambridge, on November 9, 1783, in spite of opposition from people who did not appreciate the young man's evangelical zeal or doctrine. The next day, Simeon preached his first sermon at the church.

The building held about nine hundred people, but most of the members stayed home in protest. Simeon preached to the visitors who came to hear him. Then the pewholders locked the doors of the pews to prevent visitors from using them. So, Simeon placed benches in the aisles; but the church officers threw the benches into the churchyard. Simeon started a Sunday evening service to reach the needy sinners, and the officers locked the church doors.

It is difficult to believe that Charles Simeon remained at Holy Trinity Church for fifty-four years, the first thirty of which were filled with constant opposition, persecution, and harassment. He was ordained September 28, 1783, and he took his ordination vows seriously. Simeon had a very high view of the ministry and was determined to do his best to be faithful, no matter what the university, the church officers, or the townsmen might do. During the first fourteen years of his ministry, he labored alone; but then he was allowed to have assistants who shared the load with him.

One of his young assistants was Henry Martyn, one of the first missionaries to India. Some years ago Henry Martyn's namesake, Dr. D. Martyn Lloyd-Jones, gave my wife and me a guided tour of Cambridge, centering on Holy Trinity Church. He enjoyed showing us the "upper room" where Martyn gave himself to Christ for service, as well as the famous pulpit from which Simeon faithfully preached the Word.

Simeon realized that it was the preaching of the Word of God alone that could change lives and change the church. In 1792, he started sermon classes for the young men who were training for ministry at the university. Since there were no special ministerial courses for students training for the church, Simeon's lectures met a real need. It was not easy for these young men to associate with Simeon, because he was an object of scorn and ridicule. They were known as Simeonites or Sims to the other students.

But God blessed Simeon's ministry, and the church began to prosper. The zealous pastor used to rise at four each morning so that he might devote hours to prayer and the study of the Bible. He himself had received no training in Bible study, sermon preparation, or pastoral ministry. He was teaching himself that he might be able to teach others, and God met his needs. His convictions about the ministry and preaching are worth considering today.

"My endeavor," he wrote, "is to bring out of Scripture what is there and not to trust in what I think might be there." He also said, "Take the Word as little children without enquiring what human system it appears to favor." Simeon made it clear that he was neither a Calvinist nor an Arminian, but rather a Bible Christian. "Be a Bible Christian and not a system Christian," he advised his students.

Of course, in Simeon's day, the great controversy over doctrine centered around John Wesley the Arminian, and George Whitefield, the Calvinist. Simeon had a delightful personal meeting with Wesley on December 20, 1784. Wesley recorded in his journal: "I went to Hinxworth, where I had the satisfaction of meeting Mr. Simeon. . . . He gave me the pleasing information, that there are three parish churches in Cambridge, wherein true scriptural religion is preached; and several young gentlemen who are happy partakers of it." But Simeon has left us with a more complete record of the conversation.

"Sir," said Simeon to Wesley, "I understand that you are called an Arminian; and I have been sometimes called a Calvinist; and therefore I suppose we are to draw daggers. But before I consent to begin the combat, with your permission I will ask you a few questions, not from impertinent curiosity, but for real instruction. Pray, Sir, do you feel yourself a depraved creature, so depraved that you would never have thought of turning to God if God had not first put it into your heart?"

"Yes, I do indeed," Wesley replied.

"And do you utterly despair of recommending yourself to

God by anything you can do; and look for salvation solely through the blood and righteousness of Christ?"

"Yes, solely through Christ."

"But, sir, supposing you were first saved by Christ, are you not somehow or other to save yourself afterwards by your own works?"

"No; I must be saved by Christ from first to last."

"Allowing then that you were first turned by the grace of God, are you not in some way or other to keep yourself by your own power?"

"No."

"What, then, are you to be upheld every hour and every moment by God, as much as an infant in its mother's arms?"

"Yes, altogether."

"And is all your hope in the grace and mercy of God to preserve you unto his heavenly kingdom?"

"Yes, I have no hope but in him."

"Then, sir, with your leave, I will put up my dagger again; for this is all my Calvinism; this is my election, my justification by faith, my final perseverance: it is, in substance, all that I hold, and as I hold it: and therefore, if you please, instead of searching out terms and phrases to be a ground of contention between us, we will cordially unite in those things wherein we agree."

Always burdened to help others preach the Word, Simeon in 1796 published a book of one hundred "skeletons" of expository sermons, and increased it to five hundred outlines five years later (he claimed that he had put over seven thousand hours of work into those five hundred outlines). He had discovered *An Essay on the Composition of Sermons* by the French preacher, Jean Claude, and had received great help from it; so he translated it and made it available to English readers.

Eventually, his little book of sermon skeletons grew into a large set of books containing 2536 outlines covering the entire Bible. His critics called these skeletons nothing but a valley of dry bones, but Charles Spurgeon recommended them. "Be a prophet," he said, "and they will live!"

As he grew in grace and in his ministry, Simeon had to battle his aristocratic nature and learn love and humility. In his early years, he was demanding and autocratic; but the Holy Spirit prevailed, and he learned to minister in love. He was orthodox in his doctrine, but he knew that orthodoxy alone was not sufficient for an effective ministry. He wrote: "True, you are not to keep back the fundamental doctrines of the Gospel: but there are different ways of stating them; and you should adopt that which expresses kindness and love, and not that which indicates an unfeeling harshness."

He saw the pastor as a combination of spiritual father, heavenly ambassador, and a watchman on the wall. He often quoted Ezekiel 33:8 and reminded his people that the minister must warn as well as encourage. The text he chose for his own epitaph was I Corinthians 2:2, and it accurately describes his ministry. "My aim in the style of preaching," he said, "is to do it so plainly and simply that all may understand and be ready to say, 'I could have made as good a sermon myself.' "

Simeon was concerned that evangelical men be assigned to the various churches, so he used his wealth to "buy up" benefices and give them to qualified men. In those days, in the Anglican Church, the buildings and ministry of various churches were actually owned by wealthy patrons, and the right to appoint the pastor could actually be purchased. Simeon set up a Patronage Trust to oversee this special ministry, and as a result, godly evangelical men were put into the churches, much to the regret of the liberal opposition.

Simeon traveled widely in Great Britain, preaching wherever the doors were open to him. He was always true to the Anglican Church, but he was open to sincere believers everywhere. He had a special burden for missions and helped to found the Church Missionary Society. He also had a burden for the Jews and came very close to a premillennial view of the future of Israel. He even founded a chapel in Amsterdam for witness to the Jews there.

In 1813, Simeon instituted what he called "conversation parties," informal Friday evening fellowships at which he would answer questions relating to the spiritual life. These parties were the means of encouraging many young Christians in the faith. He also started summer "house parties" for clergymen and their wives, to give them opportunity for relaxation combined with spiritual fellowship and encouragement. Simeon might well be considered the father of the summer pastoral institute program.

In 1832, Simeon commemorated the fiftieth anniversary of his ministry, and by this time he had either silenced or outlasted all his enemies. He gave a dinner for several hundred of the poorer churchgoers, received congratulations from many famous people, and preached a stirring sermon from II Peter 1:12–15. There was harmony in the church, the buildings were being renovated, and the Gospel was going forth with clarity and power. He had come a long way from those days when his church officers had locked him out of his own church.

It was the courageous preaching of the Word of God that had brought about the change. Simeon wrote that his test for preaching was: Does it humble the sinner? Does it exalt the Savior? Does it promote holiness? Critics might call his twenty-one volumes of outlines dead skeletons, but they throbbed with life when he preached them. At one service, a little girl asked her mother, "Mama, what is the gentleman in a passion about?" The answer: He was in a passion to proclaim Jesus Christ and him crucified.

Charles Simeon died, honored and full of days, on November 13, 1836. Even though it was market day, the town closed all the shops for his funeral, and the university canceled all lectures. Nearly two thousand people, including the robed academic community, paid tribute to the man who had remained true to the Word during fifty-four years of difficult ministry. The people would not hear his voice again, but the word that he preached would go on, and the men he had influenced and trained would continue the ministry.

Charles Simeon, by Handley Moule (Inter-Varsity Press), is a warm biography written by a Bible scholar sympathetic to Simeon's position. A more recent work is *Charles Simeon of*

Cambridge by Hugh Evan Hopkins (Eerdmans). If you want to read some of his university sermons, secure *Let Wisdom Judge,* edited by Arthur Pollard and published by Inter-Varsity Press. Simeon's Bible outlines were reprinted some years ago by Zondervan but are now out of print.

What does Charles Simeon say to us today, even those of us who might not totally agree with his views of the church? For one thing, preach the Word. For another, stay with the job in spite of opposition. He would also urge us to reproduce ourselves in others so that the ministry might continue and grow. Finally, he would set the example for disciplined prayer and study. He spent the first four hours of every day with God, and he grew because of it.

The aristocrat in the pulpit was truly an ambassador from God.

11

One-Eyed Preacher from the North

Johanna Evans gave birth to a son on December 25, 1766; so she and her husband, Samuel, decided to name him Christmas. Their humble home was in Llandyssul, Cardiganshire, Wales, a land of wild scenery and fiery preaching. Little did they know that their boy would grow up to become one of the greatest pulpit masters Wales would produce.

Samuel died while Christmas was a child, so his mother sent him to the farm of her brother, James Lewis. Christmas remained there for six miserable years. Lewis was a cruel man and a drunkard. Christmas received no education—at seventeen he could neither read nor write—and no moral or religious training. He was repeatedly involved in fights; only the providence of God kept him from being killed. Once he was stabbed, and once he nearly drowned. In one of these brawls he lost his right eye; for the remainder of his life he had to daub the empty socket with laudanum to ease the pain.

When Christmas was seventeen, he left the farm and went to work for a Presbyterian minister. He was caught up in a revival in the church and was soundly converted. Within a short time he learned to read and write, and he even began to minister in a small way. In those days it was customary to hold cottage meetings for the poorer people, and Evans used to occasionally preach or pray. He later admitted that he memorized sermons and prayers that he found in books.

As he studied his Bible, his religious convictions changed, and in 1786 he joined the Baptist church. So effective was his ministry of the Word that the church ordained him in 1790 and sent him to an area where the work was small and struggling. He took his bride to Lleyn, trusted God, and saw a time of rich blessing.

The preaching tradition in Wales is a very strong one. In those days, huge crowds of people attended preaching festivals to hear men declare the Word of God. These annual gatherings would draw as many as twenty-five thousand people into the natural amphitheaters. The Welsh people have poetry, song, and preaching in their blood. And the more dramatic and imaginative the preaching, the better they like it.

Christmas Evans first came into prominence at a Baptist Association preaching festival. The crowd was waiting for two of their spell-binding preachers to show up when someone suggested that it would be a good thing to warm up the crowd so they would be ready. One of the ministers suggested, "Why not ask the one-eyed lad from the North? I hear he preaches quite wonderfully." Christmas Evans instantly agreed to preach and took Colossians 1:21 as his text.

One of the traditions of Welsh preaching is "catching the *hwyl*." I once discussed this subject with the late Dr. D. Martyn Lloyd-Jones, himself a Welshman and a master preacher. He explained that the Welsh word *hwyl* means "the canvas of a ship." In preaching it refers to "catching the wind of the Spirit" and being carried along with great spiritual power. Often the preacher would move the crowds by raising his voice to a high-pitched falsetto—"oratory on fire"—as he was caught up in the power and unction of the Spirit.

Christmas Evans caught the *hwyl* that day. The people began to move closer to the preacher, amazed that the tall, bony, ill-dressed farm youth had such power with words and over people. He was the talk of the festival, the newest preaching sensation in Wales.

In 1792 Evans and his wife moved to the Island of Anglesea (or Anglesey) in Northwest Wales; there he ministered for twenty years. When he arrived, there were ten small Baptist societies meeting, some of them torn apart over religious controversies. Evans rode his horse from meeting to meeting and eventually developed twenty preaching places where people eagerly assembled to hear him. Within a few years, he saw more than six hundred people trust Christ and enter the family of God.

Twice in his long life Christmas Evans made a special covenant with God. The first time was on April 10, 1802. It was a solemn covenant of dedication, with thirteen paragraphs spelling out his personal commitment to Jesus Christ. He signed each paragraph "Amen. C.E." It is touching to read this covenant and to realize that God honored his faith and dedication.

Christmas Evans was a self-taught man. He taught himself Hebrew and Greek, and he read the meaty works of men like John Owen and John Gill. Though he had but one eye, he was a constant reader, either in his simple home or while riding to a preaching appointment. He often preached daily and twice on Sunday, and while he was riding, he meditated and wrote his eloquent sermons.

Mrs. Evans died in 1823, and in 1826 Christmas Evans remarried, resigned from the Anglesea ministry and accepted a small Baptist church in Tonyvelin, in Caerphilly. Unfortunately, the jealousy of younger ministers and the barbs of theological controversy were damaging the work in Anglesea, and Evans felt it was time to move. The problems are reflected in the second covenant that Evans made with the Lord on April 24, 1829.

As he was returning home from a preaching mission, a spirit of prayer came upon him, and he stopped to commune with God, weep, and pray. He wrote fifteen requests of God and signed each one "Amen. C.E." Here are a few quotations:

Grant Thy blessing upon bitter things, to brighten and quicken me, more and more, and not to depress and make me more lifeless.

Suffer me not to be trodden under the proud feet of members, or deacons, for the sake of Thy goodness.

Help me to wait silently, and patiently upon Thee, for the fulfillment of these things, and not become enraged, angry, and speak unadvisedly with my lips, like Moses, the servant of the Lord. Sustain my heart from sinking, to wait for fresh strength from Zion.

God gave him a new experience of faith and power, even though the enemy opposed the preaching of the Word. In 1832, he made his final move and became pastor of a dying church at Caernarvon where thirty members were struggling under the weight of a debt they could not pay.

Evans wrote in his journal: "I have been thinking of the great goodness of the Lord unto me, throughout my unworthy ministry; and now, in my old age, I see the work prospering wonderfully in my hand, so that there is reason to think that I am, in some degree, a blessing to the Church."

When he had been at the chapel six years, Evans, his wife, and a young pastor set out on a preaching mission to raise funds to pay off the crippling debt. He put a notice in the *Welsh Magazine* asking his brethren to pray for and support this special endeavor. "This is my last sacrifice for the Redeemer's cause," he wrote, and it was. But God prospered the mission and great crowds heard him preach; even when the meeting house was filled crowds stood outside and listened.

But the undertaking was too difficult for the old preacher. On Sunday, July 15, he preached two sermons in Swansea, in the morning on the Prodigal Son, and in the evening on Romans 1:16. He preached again on Monday on a favorite text, "and beginning at Jerusalem." When he concluded the message, he said in a quiet voice, "This is my last sermon." He became ill the next day; and on Friday, July 20, 1838, Christmas Evans was called to Glory. His last words were, "Goodbye! Drive on!"

Christmas Evans often counseled younger pastors, and his philosophy of ministry is worth sharing today. He wrote to one: "Consider, in the first place, the great importance, to a preacher, of a blameless life." Then he added, "I remember the words of Luther, that *reading, prayer,* and *temptation* are necessary to strengthen, and to purify the talents of a minister."

We expect him to give this advice: "Always have a book to read, instead of indulging in vain conversations. Strive to learn English. . . . Remember this, that you cannot commit some loved sin in private, and perform the work of the ministry in public, with facility and acceptance."

Evans could preach with power both in English and Welsh, and in both languages his aim was to honor Christ. "The gospel, as a glass, shuld be kept clean and clear in the pulpit," he wrote, "that the hearers may see the glory of Christ and be changed to the same image."

When asked about style and delivery, Evans said, "Preach the Gospel of the grace of God intelligently, affectionately, and without shame— all the contents of the great box, from predestination to glorification. . . . Let the preacher influence himself; let him reach his own heart, if he would reach the hearts of others; if he would have others feel, he must feel himself."

Evans liked to compare the ministry of the Word to that of a miner, who takes the ore from the earth, melts it, and puts it into the mold. "The Gospel is like a form, or mold, and sinners are to be melted, as it were, and cast into it." He urged younger preachers to be faithful to "the form of sound words" that Paul wrote about (II Tim. 1:13).

With all of his reputation for pulpit eloquence and evangelistic zeal, Evans should perhaps be remembered most as a man of prayer. He never worried about the theology or philosophy of prayer; he simply prayed, and God answered. He had three stated times for prayer during the day, and he regularly arose at midnight to seek the face of God. He enjoyed the solitude of his long journeys, when he could pray and meditate on the deep things of God. The passion in his preaching arose from the burning in his heart.

From a human point of view, Christmas Evans seemed an unlikely candidate for becoming a spiritual giant. Born and raised in poverty, subjected to brutality, deprived of formal education, lacking in the physical graces that usually attract others, this child of Wales was certainly a trophy of the grace of God. Deaf to the slanders of his enemies and blind to the obstacles around him, he courageously and sacrificially carried the Gospel throughout the land, and many found salvation because of his ministry.

During his long and difficult ministry, he never received large salaries. He could have carved out a religious empire for himself, but he preferred to follow the Lord into the small and difficult places where men needed the bread of life. Instead of embroiling himself in the hairsplitting theological discussions and controversies of the day, he gave himself to the preaching of the Gospel and the great truths that undergird that saving message.

In short, Christmas Evans was a man of God who gave himself unsparingly to the work of the ministry. God used him to bring life to dead sinners, to dead churches, and to Christians whose spiritual experience was dead.

"Life is the only cure for death," he said, "Not the prescriptions of duty, not the threats of punishment and damnation, not the arts and refinements of education, but new, spiritual, Divine *Life*."

Perhaps that is the prescription we most need today.

12

Apostle of Certainty

"Young man, you had better get to work for the Lord!"

D. L. Moody, during his New Haven campaign of 1878, addressed that statement to a Yale Divinity School senior who had asked him about winning souls to Christ. That student was Reuben Archer Torrey, and, to Torrey's credit, he stayed around long enough to learn how to win the lost to Christ. Moody gave the students some verses to use in soul-winning and then said, "Now, gentlemen, go at it!"

At the meetings Torrey saw a young lady he had met at a dance prior to his own conversion, so he decided to try out his evangelistic skill on her. It took two hours of answering questions and referring to Scripture, but she finally yielded to the Lord and became the first convert of the man who would eventually win thousands to Christ in his worldwide ministry.

R. A. Torrey was born in Hoboken, N.J., January 28, 1856, the son of a well-to-do banker. The family was associated with the Congregational Church, but only the mother was a true believer. It was her prayer that her son would become a minister of the Gospel, but Reuben decided he wanted to be a lawyer. However, deep within, he had the haunting feeling that God had indeed called him to be a preacher; yet he was not even a professed Christian.

One night he had a vivid dream that his mother was dead. Suddenly, she appeared in his room in the form of an angel and begged him to give himself to the ministry. In the dream he promised her that he would do so, but in his waking hours, the prospects of going to Yale University excited him so much that the impact of the dream faded from his mind.

He entered Yale in 1871 and soon found himself caught up in what his mother would have called worldly living: gambling at cards, drinking, dancing, and smoking. Chapel was compulsory but not very exciting spiritually, and even though Reuben attended church faithfully on Sundays, read his Bible daily, and kept up the image of being a Christian, he knew he was far from the Kingdom.

At the end of his sophomore year he faced the crisis. His worldly life did not satisfy him, he was not really "making it" on campus (his choice fraternity did not elect him), and he was still haunted by the feeling that God had called him to preach. One night he became so despondent and desperate that he decided to commit suicide. He reached for his razor, but God arrested him; and, instead, Torrey fell to his knees and prayed: "God, if you will take away this awful burden, I will preach!" God lifted the burden, God's peace filled his heart, and he fell sound asleep and woke up the next morning knowing that he was in God's hands.

What brought about the change? Torrey explained: "My mother, 427 miles away, was praying and praying that I would become a minister of the Gospel. And though I had gotten over sermons and arguments and churches and everything else, I could not get over my mother's prayers."

He entered Yale Divinity School in 1875. In 1877. both of his parents died within three weeks of each other. Unfortunately, the Torrey estate had all but disappeared during the panic of seventy-three, so Reuben was not made a wealthy man by his father's death. "I'm glad I did not inherit a fortune," he said later. "It would have ruined me."

While he was at Divinity School, Torrey first met D. L. Moody and learned from him how to win souls. Torrey graduated in 1878, and on November 9 of that year he became pastor of the Congregational Church in Garrettsville, Ohio, population 969. He was still rather ignorant of the Bible, but he devoted his morning hours to concentrated study. Gifted by the Lord with a brilliant mind, Torrey learned rapidly and tried to practice and share what he learned. The church prospered, and he even found himself a bride and was married October 22, 1879.

Torrey might have remained in pastoral ministry were it not for Howard Bell, a wealthy Yale classmate, who urged him to study in Germany and even offered to pay the expenses. Torrey refused his generous gift, but he did accept a loan; and in the fall of 1882 he sailed for Europe with his wife and little daughter. He divided his time between the universities in Leipzig and Erlangen, studying under such famous scholars as Franz Delitzsch and Theodore Zahn. That year of concentrated study further convinced him that the "old faith" was true and that the message of the Gospel was the only hope for a lost world.

When he returned to the United States, he had two invitations for ministry: a wealthy church in Brooklyn, and a small group of believers in Minneapolis who wanted to begin a new ministry. Torrey decided for Minneapolis. There he threw himself into personal evangelism, preaching, and teaching. He organized the People's Church (Congregational) and rejoiced in the blessings God gave.

In 1906, Torrey led a sixteen-year-old lad to Christ, and that lad, Oswald J. Smith, would one day organize the People's Church in Toronto.

During his years of ministry and study in Minneapolis, Torrey reached some definite conclusions about doctrinal matters. Trained as a lawyer, he knew that all the evidence he needed was in the Bible, and he was willing to accept all that the Bible taught. For one thing, he became a convinced premillennialist, and all his life he preached the blessed hope of the Lord's return. He also became an immersionist, but he never made baptism a test of fellowship. His study of Scripture also convinced him of the doctrine of eternal punishment.

Two doctrinal matters that in later years gave him some trouble with other conservative believers were divine healing and the baptism of the Spirit. While Torrey did not believe in healers, with all of their religious promotion, he did believe in "the prayer of faith" (James 5:14–15) and personally experienced healing from God. He often prayed for others, and they were healed.

In all his ministry, Torrey emphasized the importance of the power of the Holy Spirit. At one point he determined not to preach again until he had been "endued with power from on high" (Luke 24:49), so he shut himself up for a week and prayed. God answered his prayer, and others could tell that God's hand was powerfully upon him. Like Moody, Torrey did not quibble over terminology, something that he probably would change if he were on the scene today. He seemed to equate "the baptism of the Spirit" with "the fullness of the Spirit."

When a friend told D. L. Moody about Torrey's ministry in Minneapolis, the evangelist said, "You make my mouth water for him!" Moody usually got what he wanted; so on September 26, 1889, R. A. Torrey began his ministry as superintendent of the Chicago Evangelization Society, later to be known as the Moody Bible Institute. Torrey developed the curriculum and made sure of the emphasis on consecration, zeal for souls, a knowledge of the Bible, and a willingness to sacrifice. In a very real sense, Torrey was the architect who made the design for every Bible institute that has been founded since his time.

From 1894 to 1906, Torrey also served as pastor of the Chicago Avenue Church, which later became the Moody Memorial Church. The building seated 2200 people, and it was usually packed at each service, with people having to sit in overflow rooms. More than two thousand members were received into the church during Torrey's ministry, and multitudes were converted. So effective was his ministry that invitations came to him from across the nation and even from other countries.

During a revival prayer meeting at the church, Torrey was

strangely led to pray that God would send him around the world and give him thousands of souls in response to the preaching of the Gospel. Shortly after, two Christians from Australia invited him to hold a campaign in Melbourne. As God provided adequate leadership both for the church and the school, Torrey felt led to accept the invitation.

On December 23, 1901, he left on the world tour, ministering in Japan, China, Australia, New Zealand, India, and Great Britain. The well-known evangelistic singer Charles Alexander joined him in Australia; and Torrey and Alexander were to become as famous a team as Moody and Sankey. The records indicate that more than one hundred thousand persons made decisions for Christ during this worldwide campaign, 1902-1905. R. A. Torrey, like D. L. Moody before him, returned to the United States to find himself a famous man.

In 1906, Torrey resigned the pastorate of the church, and two years later, resigned from the school. On February 8, 1908, he helped to found the Bible Institute of Los Angeles (BIOLA) and served as dean from 1912 to 1924. On September 3, 1915, he became founding pastor of the Church of the Open Door in Los Angeles, starting with eighty-six charter members. He also assisted in establishing the Testimony Publishing Company, funded by the Stewart brothers of Union Oil fame. This new company published *The Fundamentals*, a series of inexpensive books that defended the faith.

Those were busy years for Torrey as he was writing, preaching, directing a school, and pastoring a church, while preaching at key conferences across the nation. In 1908 he had organized the Montrose Bible Conference at Montrose, Pennsylvania, and this soon became a meeting place for hungry Christians eager to study the Bible. By 1924 he felt that he needed to slow down, so he resigned from all his ministries and "retired" to Asheville, North Carolina. He then teamed up with Homer Hammontree and went out on the evangelistic circuit again.

He held his last campaign in the First Presbyterian Church, Orlando, Florida, November 28—December 11, 1927. He be-

gan to experience throat trouble and had to cancel all his meetings. He spent the summer at his beloved Montrose, unable to
participate in any personal ministry. At the close of the season,
he returned to Asheville, and there he died on October 26,
1928. The funeral was at Montrose, and he was buried on beautiful Sunset Knoll.

Some years ago I heard an eloquent preacher tell several
thousand Christians that they had to make a choice between
serving God as "deep Bible teachers" or as soul-winners. If Reuben Archer Torrey had been in that meeting, he would have
protested. He himself was a man with a keen mind, a profound
ability to teach the Word, and a sincere burden for the lost.
His studies in Germany gave him the weapons to fight German
higher criticism and theological liberalism. He had wrestled
with theological problems and found the answers in the infal-
lible Word of God.

But Torrey was a *balanced* man; in fact, he was a man who
seemed to have everything. He was a powerful evangelist and
also a concerned pastor. He was an educator and yet a stirring
teacher. His books are still published and are exerting a lasting
influence in the lives of new generations of Christians. His most
recent biographer, Roger Martin, calls R. A. Torrey the apostle
of certainty. He stood like a giant at a time when winds of
doctrine were blowing against the church and causing people
to stumble and fall. In Reuben Archer Torrey, God proved once
again that education and evangelism, depth and soulwinning,
need not destroy one another. If a man is submitted to the
Word and filled with the Spirit, he can have an enlightened
mind and a burning heart, and he can reach people for Christ.

How to Work for Christ and *What the Bible Teaches* are perhaps Torrey's most treasured books, and they are still available. You will also want to read his books on prayer and the
Holy Spirit. *How to Succeed in the Christian Life* is excellent
for new believers. *R. A. Torrey: Apostle of Certainty*, by Roger
Martin, is published by The Sword of the Lord Publishers and
is worth reading.

During his British campaign, Torrey said to a vast audience:

"I would rather win souls than be the greatest king or emperor on earth; I would rather win souls than be the greatest general that ever commanded an army. . . . My one ambition in life is to win as many as possible. Oh, it is the only thing worth doing, to save souls; and men and women, we can all do it."

D. L. Moody started it all when he said, "Young man, you had better get to work for the Lord!"

Perhaps the Lord is saying the same thing *to you*.

13

George Whitefield— Assistant to All

"O Heavenly Father," prayed a twenty-two-year-old preacher in London, "for Thy dear Son's sake, keep me from climbing."

That young preacher was George Whitefield, and he had every reason to fear popularity and promotion. Great crowds were coming to hear him preach the Gospel, and hundreds were being converted to faith in Christ. He was the boy wonder of London. His preaching shook both Great Britain and the United States, and the results are still with us.

Historians tell us that Whitefield preached from forty to sixty hours a week, a total of more than eighteen thousand sermons during thirty-four years of public ministry. He crossed the Atlantic thirteen times and ministered extensively in the American colonies. He preached to thousands throughout Great Britain, and this included three trips to Ireland and fourteen visits to Scotland.

"I had rather wear out than rust out," he told a friend who protested that he preached too often. He often quoted the adage, "We are immortal until our work is done." When you realize that Whitefield was not a healthy man, that he often

had severe spells of vomiting, and that he arose each morning
at four o'clock, this record of ministry becomes even more
amazing.

We need to meet this boy preacher whom Dr. D. Martyn
Lloyd-Jones called the greatest preacher that England has ever
produced.

George Whitefield was born in Gloucester on December 16,
1714, into a respectable family that owned and managed the
Bell Inn. Whitefield was but two years old when his father
died, and when his mother remarried eight years later, the
match was an unhappy one.

Young George had a good memory and a glib tongue, so he
excelled in making speeches in school and acting in plays. Little did he realize that his youthful public appearances would
help to prepare him for his pulpit ministry.

Of course, as a youngster, he got involved in the usual sins
of youth, even to the point of stealing money from his mother.
But even in the midst of his childhood corruption (as he termed
it), he had the conviction that he would one day be a clergyman. "I was always fond of being a clergyman," he wrote in
his *Journal*, and "used frequently to imitate the ministers reading prayers, etc."

When he was about fifteen, he left school to assist his mother
in the work of the inn. He continued to read the Bible even
though he was not a professed Christian, and during a visit
with his brother in Bristol, he found great delight in attending
church. He made vows and apparently had some adolescent
emotional religious experiences; but no sooner had he returned
to Gloucester than the old life overtook him again.

By the providence of God, Whitefield did return to school
and then entered Oxford, where he met John and Charles Wesley and became a part of their Holy Club. While the Wesley
brothers and their friends were moral and religious people,
they did not as yet know much about the new birth. Their
Christianity consisted mainly of religious exercises, mutual
exhortation and ministry to the poor and needy.

John Wesley gave Whitefield a copy of Henry Scrougal's

spiritual classic, *The Life of God in the Soul of Man;* and the reading of that book opened Whitefield's eyes to the miracle of the new birth (at that time, Wesley himself knew nothing of a regeneration experience). Whitefield did not enter into true life and liberty immediately, but at least he was moving in the right direction. Finally, in the spring of 1735, he cast himself on God's mercy and experienced the new life in Christ.

He returned to Gloucester, where he lived with friends for several months. He began there his lifelong practice of reading the Bible on his knees and studying his Greek New Testament (Whitefield was a competent Greek and Latin student). He also purchased the famous *Matthew Henry Commentary* and read it carefully. In fact, the set became his constant companion in all his travels.

He gathered around him a small group of new believers, many of them his old "partners in crime," and they met weekly for Bible study, prayer, and mutual edification. This was the first Methodist Society ever to be organized. It comes as a surprise to many people to learn that it was George Whitefield, not John and Charles Wesley, who founded the Methodist Church. The Wesleys entered into Whitefield's labors and eventually were given the leadership of the movement by Whitefield.

Whitefield returned to Oxford in March 1736. The Wesleys had already sailed to Georgia to work with General Oglethorpe in the new colony. On June 10, 1736, George Whitefield was ordained deacon by Bishop Martin Benson in Gloucester; and on June 26, he preached his first sermon. The curious congregation—many of them relatives and friends—were amazed at the power and spiritual wisdom of the young preacher. In fact, someone reported to the bishop that Whitefield's sermon "drove fifteen people mad." The bishop said he hoped the madness would not be forgotten by the next Sunday.

That was the beginning of a miracle ministry. In July, Whitefield graduated from Oxford; and for the next two months, he ministered in London as supply preacher for a friend. He then preached for four months in Oxford, followed by a marvelous ministry in Gloucester, Bristol, and London. Thousands came to listen, and hundreds were brought to the Savior. He personally counseled with hundreds of seeking souls. Wherever he preached, the crowds were great and the benefits were lasting.

On February 1, 1738, John Wesley returned from Georgia, a weary and defeated man. His ministry in the colony had been a failure; and, unfortunately, he had left behind a bad name and a number of determined enemies. Whitefield had felt a call to serve in Georgia, and he was ready to sail when Wesley's ship arrived in England.

For some reason, Wesley did not try to see Whitefield personally; but he did try to persuaded him not to go to Georgia. In his earlier years, John Wesley believed in casting lots to determine God's will for himself and for his friends. Had Whitefield listened to Wesley at that time, what a loss it would have been to the people of the United States. On February 2, 1738, Whitefield set off on the first of seven visits to the colonies, visits that were greatly blessed of God and helped to spearhead the Great Awakening.

Whitefield arrived at Savannah, Georgia, on May 7. The very next day, in London, John Wesley "very unwillingly" attended that meeting in Aldersgate Street where his heart was "strangely warmed," and he found the assurance of personal salvation through faith in Christ. He then began to preach the Word and gradually enter into the ministries that Whitefield had left behind.

Whitefield returned to London in December and found himself excluded from all but four London churches. He preached again to thousands and experienced a mighty working of the Spirit. He and the Wesleys joined forces in the sharing of the Gospel. On January 14, 1739, Whitefield was ordained a priest of the Church of England; throughout his ministry, he remained true to those ordination vows. Though his ministry was interdenominational, he was always a faithful son of the Church of England.

Finding that he was excluded from the established churches, Whitefield decided to take to the open air; on February 17, he began his outdoor preaching at Kingswood near Bristol. "It was a brave day for England when Whitefield began field preaching!" Charles Spurgeon told his students. Whitefield collected the miners and their families, about two hundred people, and preached the Gospel to them. "Blessed be God!" said the evangelist, "I have now broken the ice!"

From that day on, wherever Whitefield set up his portable pulpit, huge crowds gathered, from among the poor and from the upper strata of English society. Even the little children crowded close to the preacher to hear him. Whitefield followed this practice both in Britain and in America. Benjamin Franklin calculated that Whitefield's message could be heard *clearly* by thirty thousand people at one time.

Whitefield began to organize societies and place mature believers over them to supervise the growth of the converts. By now, John Wesley was also preaching in the open air, following Whitefield's example; and the movement took on the name Methodist, from the Holy Club that had been founded at Oxford.

Both the preachers and the converts were persecuted by the unbelieving rabble, sometimes with the approval of the resident clergy. It was not unusual for Wesley and Whitefield to be pelted with stones and dirt, or worse, or to have a dead cat hurled at their heads. But, like the apostles of old, none of these things moved them, and they continued to preach the Word and organize societies.

Whitefield had two reasons to be interested in America. One was the preaching of the Word, and the other was the founding and managing of an orphan's home in Georgia. While preaching in Britain, he often took an offering for the home; and he also encouraged his many American friends to support it. For a long time, the home was a heavy burden on the evangelist, and it probably cost him more in health, time, and energy than it was worth. At one point he was afraid of being arrested for the debts incurred by the home. Whenever he visited the colonies, he always made his way to Georgia to check on the work, supervise some construction, and encourage the workers. The spiritual influence of George Whitefield on colonial America can never be fully estimated.

It is no secret that John and Charles Wesley were Arminian in doctrine, while Whitefield was more Calvinistic. The Wesleys opposed the doctrines of election, predestination, and the security of the believer. One day, Charles Wesley called John Calvin "the firstborn son of the Devil!" Whitefield begged the Wesleys not to bring their doctrinal differences into the pulpit, but the men refused to listen. While Whitefield was ministering in America, John Wesley published his sermon on "Free Grace" in which he openly attacked Whitefield's theology.

This painful conflict ultimately divided the Methodists and led to the founding of a Calvinistic Methodist branch, which was particularly strong in Wales. Like most disputes, there were faults and mistakes on both sides, because even the most saintly men are made of clay. Wesley's emphasis on Christian perfection irritated Whitefield; and Whitefield's proclamation of the doctrines of grace upset Wesley.

However, it is to Whitefield's credit that he strenuously sought reconciliation and fellowship with the Wesleys. He did his utmost to keep the controversy private. Finally, Whitefield did the one thing his friends had hoped he would not do: He turned the entire ministry over to Wesley and stepped aside as leader. "I have no party to be at the head of," he wrote, "and through God's grace I will have none; but as much as in me lies, I will strengthen the hands of all of every denomination that preach Jesus Christ in sincerity."

When his followers protested his decision, he said, "Let my name be forgotten, let me be trodden under the feet of all men, if Jesus may thereby be glorified. . . . Let us look above names and parties; let Jesus be our all in all. . . . I care not who is uppermost. I know my place . . . even to be the servant of all."

He sent a letter to the godly Lady Huntingdon in which he said, "Oh, that I may learn from all I see to desire to be nothing and to think it my highest privilege to be an assistant to all but the head of none."

Whitefield spent the rest of his days as "an assistant to all."

The more popular he became, the more the opposition grew and the slanders increased. He was even mimicked on the London stage, and obscene songs were written about him. He ignored them all and continued to magnify Jesus Christ. The opposition of the unbelievers did not pain him as much as the division of the believers. "But, oh! that division!" he wrote. "What slaughter it has made!"

Early in his Christian life and ministry, Whitefield developed a love for all of God's people who held to the fundamental doctrines of the faith. When he was only twenty, he wrote in his *Journal:* "I bless God, the partition wall of bigotry and sect-religion was soon broken down in my heart; for, as soon as the love of God was shed abroad in my soul, I loved all, of whatsoever denomination, who loved the Lord Jesus in sincerity of heart."

It was during his seventh visit to America, on September 30, 1770, that George Whitefield died, in the Presbyterian parsonage at Newburyport, Massachusetts. He is buried there at the church.

The fact that Whitefield preached in the open air to crowds of thirty thousand and even forty thousand people is of itself astounding. He was the true founder of the Methodist Church, and yet he handed his leadership to another in order to preserve "the unity of the Spirit in the bond of peace." He raised great amounts of money for the care of orphans and the poor, and he helped to establish several educational institutions.

But perhaps greater than all these accomplishments is the life of the man himself. Spurgeon commented: "Often as I have read his life, I am conscious of distinct quickening whenever I turn to it. *He lived.* Other men seem to be only half alive; but Whitefield was all life, fire, wing, force. My own model, if I may have such a thing in due subordination to my Lord, is George Whitefield; but with unequal footsteps must I follow in his glorious track."

I suggest that you secure the recent two-volume biography of George Whitefield written by Arnold A. Dallimore and published by Crossway Books, a division of Good News Publishers.

Do not permit the size of the books to frighten you. These volumes read like an exciting tale of adventure; they are not in the least dull and academic. This is probably the most scholarly, and yet the most readable, biography of an evangelical preacher to appear in many years. You will learn a great deal of church history and a have a better grasp of the situation today, after reading these volumes.

Then, secure *Whitefield's Journals,* published by Banner of Truth Trust. You may even want to read the *Journals* as you read the biography. Its pages are filled with spiritual nuggets that cannot help but enrich your own spiritual life.

One final word: Pastor Dallimore devoted thirty years of his life to researching and writing this monumental biography. We are greatly indebted to him. Perhaps there is a young pastor reading this book who has the interest and ability to invest the next twenty or thirty years of his life to researching the life of Charles Spurgeon and then writing an equally readable and scholarly biography. It is long overdue.

14

Everybody's Expositor

"Suitable to everybody, instructive to all" is the way Charles Spurgeon described what is probably the best-known commentary on the Bible written in the English language, *Matthew Henry's Commentary*. Since it was published more than two hundred fifty years ago, this commentary has appeared in many different editions, including a condensation in one volume.

Spurgeon recommended that every minister of the Gospel read straight through *Matthew Henry's Commentary* at least once during his lifetime. Perhaps he got this idea from his model, George Whitefield, who carried his set of Matthew Henry on all of his travels and read it daily on his knees.

Matthew Henry was born at Broad Oaks, Shropshire, England, on October 18, 1662. His father, Philip Henry, was a Nonconformist minister who, along with two thousand other clergymen, had been ejected from his church by the Act of Uniformity issued that year by Charles II. These courageous men had refused to compromise their convictions and give "unfeigned consent and assent" to the Prayer Book. They also refused to submit to Episcopal ordination.

Philip Henry had married the heiress of a large estate in

Broad Oaks, Katherine Matthews. Her father was not in favor
of the match and told his daughter, "Nobody knows where he
came from." But the daughter wisely replied, "True, but I know
where he is going, and I should like to go with him!"

Matthew was physically weak, but it was not long before
his strength of intellect and character made themselves known.
At the age of three, he was reading the Bible; by the time he
was nine, he was competent in Latin and Greek. He spent his
first eighteen years being tutored at home, in an atmosphere
that was joyfully and lovingly Christian.

He loved to hear his father preach. A sermon on Psalm 51:17
first awakened in young Matthew a desire to know the Lord
personally. He was only ten years old at the time, but the
impression was lasting. When he was thirteen, Matthew wrote
an amazingly mature analysis of his own spiritual condition,
a document that reads like an ordination paper. Often, after
hearing his father preach, Matthew would hurry to his room
and pray that God would seal the Word and the spiritual
impressions made so that he might not lose them. God answered those youthful prayers.

In July 1680, Matthew was sent to London to study with
"that holy, faithful minister," Thomas Doolittle, who had an
academy in his home. Unfortunately, the religious persecu-
tions of that day forced Doolittle to close his academy; so Matthew returned to Broad Oaks. In April 1685, he returned to
London to study law at Gray's Inn. He was a good student, but
he never lost the burning desire to be a minister of the Gospel.

A year later, he returned to Broad Oaks and began to preach
whenever opportunity presented itself; and on May 9, 1687, he
was ordained. Before his ordination, he put himself through
a heartsearching self-examination in which he seriously studied his own Christian experience, motives for ministry, and
fitness for service. The paper contains both confession of faith
and confession of sin. He concluded that he was not entering
the ministry "as a trade to live by" or to make a name for
himself. He also concluded, "I have no design in the least to
maintain a party, or to keep up any schismatical faction."

Throughout his ministry, Matthew Henry loved and cooperated with all who trusted Christ and who wanted to serve him, no matter what their denominational connections. Even the leaders of the Episcopal Church admitted that Matthew Henry was a good and godly man. This document ought to be read by every prospective minister before he comes to ordination, and it would not hurt those of us who are already ordained to review it on occasion.

A group of believers in Chester invited Matthew Henry to become their pastor, and on June 2, 1687, he began twenty-five happy years of ministry among them. Though he was in demand to preach in other churches in the area, he was rarely absent from his own pulpit on the Lord's Day.

In August of the same year, he was married. On February 14, 1689, his wife died in childbirth, although, by the mercy of God, the daughter lived. Matthew married again on July 8, 1690, and God gave him and his wife nine children, eight of them girls, three of whom died during their first year. His only son, Philip, was born May 3, 1700, but he did not follow his father's faith, or his grandfather's. His interests lay in this world and not in the world to come.

God blessed the ministry in Chester so that a new sanctuary was erected and was dedicated on August 8, 1700. The effectiveness of Matthew Henry's pulpit ministry reached even to London, and several churches there tried to secure his services. But he loved his people at Trinity Church, Chester, and refused each invitation.

Matthew was usually in his study before five o'clock each morning, devoting himself to the preparation of his exposition of the word. He had breakfast with his family and always led them in worship, reading and expounding some passage from the Old Testament. He then returned to his study until afternoon, when he would set out to visit his people. After the evening meal, he would again lead the household in worship, using a New Testament passage for his meditation. He often questioned the children and the servants to make sure they had understood the teaching.

Often in the late evening, he would put in a few more hours of study before retiring. "Take heed of growing remiss in your work," he warned fellow pastors. "Take pains while you live. . . . The Scripture still affords new things, to those who search them." It was not unusual for him to preach seven times a week, and yet he was always fresh and practical. "No place is like my own study," he said. "No company like good books, especially the book of God." We wonder what Matthew Henry would think of those ministers who rush about all week, wasting time, and then "borrow" another man's sermon for the Lord's Day.

The key date in Matthew Henry's life is November 12, 1704; on that day he started writing his famous *Commentary*. On April 17, 1714, he completed his comments on the Book of Acts; but two months later, on June 22, he suddenly took ill and died.

Matthew Henry was not pastoring in Chester when he was called Home. On May 18, 1712, he had begun his new ministry at Hackney, in London. One of the factors that motivated his move was his desire to be closer to his publisher as his *Commentary* was being imprinted. He had ministered twenty-five years at Trinity Church, Chester, and only two years in London. The funeral service was held on June 25, and he was buried at Trinity Church.

Much of the material in Henry's *Commentary* came from his own expositions of Scripture given at family worship and from the pulpit. There is also a great deal of Philip Henry in these pages, especially the pithy sayings that season the exposition. Matthew's purpose in writing the *Commentary* was practical, not academic. He simply wanted to explain and apply the Word of God in language the common people could understand.

Several of his pastor friends gathered up his notes and sermons and completed the *Commentary* from Romans to Revelation. When you read their expositions, you can see how far short they fall of the high standard set by the original author. In true Puritan fashion, Matthew Henry had the ability to get to the heart of a passage, outline the passage clearly, and then

apply its truths to daily life. True, there were times when he
spiritualized a text and missed the point; but generally speaking, he did his work well. One does not have to agree with all
of his interpretations to benefit from his observations.

In 1765, John Wesley published an edited version of the
Commentary, hoping to bring it within the reach of the average
Christian reader. He felt it was too large and too expensive.
But, at the same time, Wesley also deleted all that Matthew
Henry had to say about election and predestination. He also
omitted an "abundance of quaint sayings" and thus took the
seasoning out of the dinner. In his preface, Wesley remarked
that he used to wonder where some preachers "whom I greatly
esteem" obtained the "pretty turns in preaching" that he heard
in their sermons; but, after reading Matthew Henry, he discovered their source. I have a suspicion that this was a gentle
criticism of his estranged friend, George Whitefield, who used
to read Matthew Henry before going into the pulpit.

You will not find Matthew Henry grappling with big problems as he expounds the Word, or always shedding light on
difficult passages in the Bible. For this kind of help you must
consult the critical commentaries. He did not know a great
deal about customs in the Holy Land, since travel to the East
was quite limited in that day. Again, the student will need up-
to-date commentaries and Bible dictionaries to help him in
that area. However, for a devotional and practical approach
to Bible exposition, this commentary leads the way.

I must confess that I have not followed Spurgeon's advice
and read straight through *Matthew Henry's Commentary;* but
I have used it with profit over the years. I think he is especially
good in Genesis, Psalms, and the four Gospels. I have never
consulted his *Commentary* early in my sermon preparation,
but rather have left him (and Maclaren and Spurgeon) until
after I had done my own digging and meditating. Often just
a sentence from Matthew Henry has opened up a new area of
thought for me and helped me feed my people.

I was surprised to discover that Matthew Henry is quoted
in our two leading books of quotations. *Bartlett's Familiar Quo-*

tations has fourteen quotations and *The Oxford Dictionary of Quotations* (3rd Edition) has six. Apparently Matthew Henry is the originator of the phrase "creature comforts" as well as the popular saying "All this and heaven too." Perhaps some enterprising reader could mine for us some of Matthew Henry's pithy sayings and put them into a book.

If you want to get to know this expositor and his father better secure *The Lives of Philip and Matthew Henry*, published by Banner of Truth. Matthew Henry wrote the biography of his father, and it is a classic. J. B. Williams wrote the son's life, but it is not as exciting.

When he was on his deathbed, Matthew Henry said to a friend, "You have been asked to take notice of the sayings of dying men—this is mine: that a life spent in the service of God and communion with Him, is the most pleasant life that anyone can live in this world."

15

Martin Luther's Rib

Since November 10, 1983, marked the five hundredth anniversary of the birth of Martin Luther, we have heard a great deal about this courageous reformer and his ministry. But I want to focus our attention now, not on Luther the preacher and leader, but on Luther the husband and father; for I want you to meet Katherine von Bora, the nun who became Martin Luther's devoted wife. He called her "Kitty, my rib," and he loved her dearly.

Katherine was born January 29, 1499, at Lippendorf, Germany, about six miles south of Leipzig. When her mother died five years later, the father put Katherine into a boarding school, and then, when she was nine, he placed her in the Cistercian convent at Nimbschen in Saxony. It was not an easy place for a little girl to grow up, but at least she had protection, food, and friends. On October 8, 1515, she was "married to Christ" and officially became a nun. Little did she realize that, two years later, a daring Wittenberg professor named Martin Luther would nail his ninety-five theses to the church door and usher in a religious movement that would change her life.

As the Reformation doctrine spread across Germany, numbers of monks and nuns became believers and sought to escape from their convents and monasteries. Some of the nuns who sought freedom were severely punished, and some who escaped were brought back into even worse bondage. Twelve nuns at the Nimbschen convent somehow got word to Luther that they wanted to get out, and he arranged for their escape.

On Easter evening, April 5, 1523, a brave merchant and his nephew, Henry and Leonard Koppe, drove a wagon load of barrels into the convent, put the twelve nuns each in a barrel, and drove away. When a suspicious man asked Koppe what he was carrying in the barrels, he replied, "Herring." Three of the girls were returned to their homes, but the other nine were taken to Wittenberg, where husbands would be found for them. Two years later all of them had husbands—except Katherine von Bora.

Luther did his best to match her with a godly husband, but all his attempts failed. The one man she really fell in love with ran off and married another girl. Luther urged her to marry Pastor Casper Glatz, but she refused. She was living with some of the leading citizens in Wittenberg and learning how to be a lady and manage a household, so those two years of waiting were not wasted. Finally, she let it be known that if Doctor Luther were to ask her to be his wife, she would not say no.

It was not that Luther was against marriage, but he knew that he was a marked man and that, if he married, he would only put his wife and family into great danger. He had urged others to marry, if only to spite the devil and his teaching (the policy of Rome concerning married clergy). How could a man who was declared a heretic by the pope and an outlaw by the Kaiser take a wife and establish a home?

But as the months passed, Luther weakened. He wrote to a friend, "If I can swing it, I'll take my Kate to wife ere I die, to spite the devil." Not the least of Luther's concerns were the economic factors involved in marriage. He accepted no payment or royalties for his books, his own income was unsteady and meager, and he was known for his generosity to anybody in need. If he wanted to deprive himself, that was one thing, but did he have the right to force his wife to make such constant sacrifices?

On June 13, 1525, Dr. Martin Luther and Katherine von Bora were married in a private ceremony at the Black Cloister, the "converted monastery" where Luther lived. As the custom was, two weeks later there was a public ceremony at the church. A host of friends attended, and the couple received many choice gifts. Of course, the enemy immediately circulated slanderous stories about the couple, but few people believed them. One man said that their first child would be the Antichrist.

Luther was forty-two years old and Katherine was twenty-five. Would the marriage succeed? History records the glorious fact that the marriage not only succeeded, but it set a high standard for Christian family life for centuries to come. The church historian Philip Schaff wrote: "The domestic life of Luther has far more than a biographical interest. It is one of the factors of modern civilization. Without Luther's reformation, clerical celibacy, with all its risks and evil consequences, might still be the universal law in all Western churches. There would be no married clergymen and clerical families in which the duties and virtues of conjugal, parental, and filial relations could be practiced. . . . Viewed simply as a husband-father, and as one of the founders of the clerical family, Luther deserves to be esteemed and honored as one of the greatest benefactors of mankind."

While we are at it, let's give some bouquets to Katherine too. It was not easy to convert a rundown cloister into a comfortable home. Nor was it easy to convert a hyperactive professor-preacher into a patient husband and father. She always called him Doctor Luther, but Luther had a number of pet names for his Katherine. "Kitty, my rib" is perhaps the best-known nickname, but he also called her *Selbander*, which is German for "better half." It was not unusual for him to refer to her as my Lord, Kate or even Doctor Katherine (she was an excellent nurse and dispenser of herb medicines). When he felt she was giving too many orders, he quietly called her *Kette*, which is the German word for "chain."

"There is a lot to get used to in the first year of marriage,"
said Luther, and no husband knew this better than he. Accustomed to planning his own day, Luther had to learn that another mind and heart were now involved in his schedule. "Wives
usually know the art to ensnare a man with tears and plead-
ings," he wrote. "They can turn and twist nicely and give the
best words."

But he had nothing to fear, for nobody was a better manager
of a house or a home than Katherine Luther. She transformed
the old cloister into a fairly comfortable house, and, like the
energetic woman of Proverbs 31, she launched into various
enterprises to feed and sustain her household. She kept cows
for milk and butter and for making cheese which, said her
guests, was better than what they purchased at the market.
She started a piggery because her husband liked pork, and this
gave Luther a new name for his wife: My Lord Kate, Mistress
of the Pigsty.

She turned a neglected field into a productive garden, and
she even planted an orchard. What produce she did not use
herself, she sold or bartered at the market and used the income
to purchase items for the home. She even stocked a pond with
fish! "Have I not at home a fair wife," Luther said proudly,
"or shall I say *boss?*"

It was not long before the Black Cloister became a crowded
and busy place. Katherine had not only her own children to
care for—six of them—but also (at various times) her own
niece and nephew, eleven of Martin's nieces and nephews, various students who boarded with them, and ever-present guests
who came to confer with her famous husband. Before the Reformation, forty monks had lived in the Cloister; now, nearly
that many joyful Christians lived there, learning to serve one
another.

Luther wisely permitted his wife to be in charge of the management of the home. To begin with, he was far too busy to
worry about such things, and, he had to admit, she did a far
better job than he could do. Katherine not only cared for him
and the household, but she ministered to the needs of people

all over Wittenberg. She listened to their problems, gave them care and medicine in their sicknesses, counseled them in their sorrows, and advised them in their business affairs. The town recognized that the Luther household was an exemplary Christian home, and much of that success was due to Katherine.

It was not easy being married to Martin Luther. He would let his food get cold while he debated theology with his guests or answered the questions of students. "Doctor," said Katherine one day as the dinner grew cold, "why don't you stop talking and eat?" Luther knew she was right, but he still snapped back, "I wish that women would repeat the Lord's Prayer before opening their mouths!" One day he said, "All my life is patience! I have to have patience with the pope, the heretics, my family, and Katie."

But out of those mealtime conversations came one of Luther's finest books. *The Table Talk of Martin Luther*. Baker Book House has reprinted the edition edited by Thomas S. Kepler, and I recommend it to you. As you read it, keep in mind that it was Katherine Luther who really made the book possible. It was at her table that these sparkling conversations were recorded—while the food grew cold.

Luther called marriage a school for character, and he was right. He realized that his own life was enriched because of the love of his wife and family. When I was teaching the history of preaching to seminary students, I reviewed Luther's philosophy of ministry and read many of his sermons, and I was impressed with the many allusions and illustrations drawn from the home. I was also impressed with Luther's Christmas sermons, and I wonder if they would have been as effective had he remained an unmarried man.

As in every home, there were times of trial and sorrow. The Luthers had six children: Hans (1526), Elizabeth (1527, died 1528), Magdalene (1529, died 1542), Martin (1531), Paul (1533), and Margaret (1534). Luther would arise at six each morning and pray with the children, and they would recite the Ten Commandments, the Creed, and the Lord's Prayer, and then sing a psalm (Luther himself was an excellent musician). He would then hurry off to preach or to lecture and would be busy the entire day.

But Luther was not a robust man, and he had many ailments that often struck him without warning. On several occasions, Katherine prepared to become a widow, but the Lord graciously healed her husband and restored him to her. In 1540, it was Katherine who was despaired of, her condition considered hopeless. Day and night her husband was at her side, praying for God's mercy on her and the children, and the Lord graciously answered. Six years later, it was Martin who was being nursed by Katherine, but his recovery was not to be, and on February 18, 1546, he entered into glory. I am sure that one of his first acts of worship in heaven was to thank God for Katherine.

Let me share two of my favorite stories about Katherine Luther.

At family devotions one morning, Luther read Genesis 22 and talked about Abraham's sacrifice of Isaac. "I do not believe it!" said Katherine. "God would not have treated his son like that!"

"But, Katie," Luther quietly replied, "He did!"

During one very difficult period, Luther was carrying many burdens and fighting many battles. Usually jolly and smiling, he was instead depressed and worried. Katherine endured this for days. One day, she met him at the door wearing a black mourning dress.

"Who died?" the professor asked.

"God," said Katherine.

"You foolish thing!" said Luther. "Why this foolishness!"

"It is true," she persisted. "God must have died, or Doctor Luther would not be so sorrowful."

Her therapy worked, and Luther snapped out of his depression.

It is interesting to read Luther's letters to his wife and note the various ways he addressed her: "To the deeply learned Mrs. Katherine Luther, my gracious housewife in Wittenberg"; "To my dear housewife, Katherine Luther, Doctress, self-martyr at

Wittenberg"; "To the holy, worrysome Lady, Katherine Luther, Doctor, at Wittenberg, my gracious, dear housewife"; "Housewife Katherine Luther, Doctress, and whatever else she may be"!

After Luther's death, the situation in Germany became critical, and war broke out. Katherine had to flee Wittenberg, and when she returned, she found her house and gardens ruined and all her cattle gone. Then the plague returned, and Katherine and the children again had to flee. During that trip, she was thrown out of a wagon into the icy waters of a ditch; and that was the beginning of the end for her. Her daughter Margaret nursed her mother tenderly, even as she had nursed others; but there was no recovery. She died on December 20, 1552, at Torgau, where she is buried in St. Mary's Church.

On her monument, you will read: "There fell asleep in God here at Torgau the late blessed Dr. Martin Luther's widow Katherine von Bora."

They could have added: "Many daughters have done virtuously, but thou excellest them all (Prov. 31:20).

I suggest that we make either January 29 or June 13 "Pastors' Wives' Day," not only in honor of Katherine von Bora, but in honor of all pastors' wives everywhere—that great host of sacrificing women of God who make it possible for their husbands to minister. I salute these women who must often turn houses into homes, who carry the burdens of their people as well as those of their own, who do without that others may have, who cheerfully bear criticism, and do it all to the glory of God.

By the way, what have *you* done lately to encourage *your* pastor's wife?

Missionary Unpredictable

Let me describe some of the things that she did, and then you answer the question: "If she were a missionary from your church, would you support Amy Carmichael?"

She spent nearly sixty years on the field and never once came home to report to her board or to the people who supported her.

While she went to the field under the authority of one board, she pretty much did her own thing and eventually started an organization of her own.

She went to the field to carry on one kind of ministry, but within a few years was carrying on an entirely different ministry that often got her into trouble with the law. At one time, she was in danger of serving seven years in prison for "assisting in the kidnapping of a child."

The reports that she sent out were often not believed by the people who read them. "Such things simply can't be!" they argued; but they were—and she proved it.

She did not ask for financial support, yet she saw every need met right on time. When people offered to sponsor part of her ministry, she suggested they support a different mission.

During the last twenty years of her ministry, she was practically an invalid, directing the work from her room.

My guess is that the average church would never have supported this kind of a missionary. She was too unpredictable,
too independent. And perhaps the average mission board would
have dropped her from their ranks after her first term. We like
the work of the ministry to be carried out in such a predictable
way that there can be no surprises, no changes, no unexpected
decisions that pioneer new territory for the Gospel. It might
upset the donors.

But Amy Carmichael was not put together that way. She
simply did not fit into our modern world of interchangeable
parts, because she was unique. She knew what God wanted
her to do, and she did it. She was not a rebel; her board and
co-laborers were full partners in the ministry. But she was one
of the Lord's special servants, and he used her to accomplish
a miracle ministry in South India.

Amy Carmichael was born on December 16, 1867, in County
Down, Northern Ireland. Her father, along with her uncle,
owned and managed several flour mills; so the family was
fairly comfortable. They came from Covenanter stock and took
the things of the Lord seriously. Amy had a happy childhood,
and, while a student at a Wesleyan Methodist school in 1883,
she trusted Christ.

Changes in the milling business forced the family to move
to Belfast. Amy's father died in 1885, and this greatly altered
both the finances and the future of the family. Mrs. Carmichael
was a woman of strong faith; in fact, much of her "apostolic
spirit" rubbed off on her daughter. One incident illustrates
this.

It was Sunday morning, and Mrs. Carmichael and the children were returning home from church. They met "a poor pa-
thetic old woman" who was burdened with a heavy bundle.
Instantly, Amy and her two brothers relieved the woman of
her bundle, took her arms, and helped her along. At first the
icy stares of the "proper Presbyterians" embarrassed them,
but then the Lord moved in and the whole scene changed.

Into Amy's mind flashed Paul's words from I Corinthians 3
about "gold, silver, precious stones, wood, hay, stubble; . . .

the fire shall try every man's work of what sort it is" (vv. 12, 13). In later years Amy wrote, "We went on. I said nothing to anyone, but I knew that something had happened that had changed life's values. Nothing could ever matter again but the things that were eternal."

In September 1886, some friends invited Amy to Glasgow, where she attended meetings along the lines of the Keswick Convention. For many months, she had been struggling with the problem of how to live a holy life; and she found the answer at the Glasgow meetings. It was not the messages of the two speakers that got through to her but the closing prayer of the chairman. He paraphrased Jude 1:24: "O Lord, we know that Thou art able to keep us from falling!" Those words brought light into the darkness, and Amy Carmichael entered into a life of faith and victory.

But holy living was not a luxury to her; it meant sacrifice and ministry. She had no time for Christians who went from meeting to meeting and soaked up Bible truth but never reached out to share Christ with others. Amy was burdened for the girls who worked in the mills, and she had already started a ministry for them at one of the local churches. But the work was growing and in some ways interfering with the church's program (Amy always was one to raise dust).

She decided that, if God wanted her to start a special work, he alone could provide the funds and the laborers; so she began to pray. Little did she realize that this experience with The Welcome (the hall that she built) would prepare her for years of ministry by faith alone. God did provide the funds, and a building was put up just for ministry to the girls at the mills. Many came to know Christ, and many were protected from lives of sin because of the influence of the ministry. This would be Amy Carmichael's emphasis for the rest of her life, to reach out to the downcast and the rejected, to love them, win them to Christ, and build them up to help others.

In later years, Amy said that there were three crises in her early life: her conversion, her entrance into the life of faith, and her call to be a missionary. That third crisis took place on

January 13, 1892, not in some dramatic way, but simply as she waited quietly before the Lord. He made it clear to her that she was to give her life to him as a missionary, and permit him to direct just as he pleased.

There were obstacles, not the least of which was her commitment to help care for elderly Robert Wilson, an old friend of the family and the chairman of the British Keswick movement. She shared these concerns with her mother and Mr. Wilson, and step by step, the Lord began to open the way. On March 3, 1893, she sailed for Japan, the first missionary sent out by the Keswick Convention.

She had some remarkable experiences in Japan, ministering through an interpreter; but Japan was not to be her permanent field. A serious illness forced her to go to China for rest, and then to Ceylon (now Sri Lanka). Can you imagine a church foreign missions committee discussing her situation and wondering if she could be trusted? By the end of 1894, she was back in England; but a year later, on November 9, 1895, she landed in India, and there she remained until her death on January 18, 1951.

Amy was under the authority of the Church of England Zenana Missionary Society, so she entered into their ministry with zeal. But she noted that many of the missionaries reported no converts, in fact, *expected* none. She also noticed that the missionary community was separated in every way from the people they were trying to reach.

While in Japan, Amy had adopted native dress (as Hudson Taylor did in China) and had sought to identify with the people. But, she had not come to India to create problems; so she went on with her work, always seeking the mind of Christ in her decisions.

Then something happened that dramatically changed Amy Carmichael's life and ministry. On March 6, 1901, little Preena, a seven-year-old girl, fled from one of the temples into the mission compound and begged to be protected. It was then that Amy uncovered one of the ugliest hidden sores on "Mother India's" body, the secret traffic in temple girls. She learned how fathers and mothers, for various selfish reasons, sold their daughters to different gods, only to turn the precious girls into temple prostitutes.

Infuriated at what Satan was doing to these dear girls, Amy declared war. How many battles she fought on her knees, wrestling for the bodies and souls of these helpless children! How many times she and her associates risked their lives, and faced arrest and imprisonment, in order to snatch some pleading child from the jaws of defilement and destruction. One by one, other girls found their way to *Amma* (the Tamil word for "mother"), and she courageously protected them. By 1904, there were seventeen children under her care, and then the Lord opened the way for them to receive and minister to babies. In 1918 they opened the boys' work, for the money-hungry idolaters sold boys to the temple gods just as they sold girls.

If you want to enter into the excitement of pioneer missions, then read Amy Carmichael's *Gold Cord*, the story of the Dohnavur Fellowship. Frank Houghton's excellent biography, *Amy Carmichael of Dohnavur*, contains many of the exciting stories that grew out of the new ministry of saving temple children. Both books are published by Christian Literature Crusade; in fact, many of Amy Carmichael's books are available from that publisher.

Amma greatly admired the work of the China Inland Mission, and, in many ways, she patterned herself after Hudson Taylor. She did not solicit funds. When people asked to have the privilege of sponsoring a child, she refused their help. All funds went into the mission account to be dispensed as the Lord directed. The many workers God brought to her side were not paid salaries, and the mission never borrowed money or went into debt. While Amy did not criticize ministries that had other policies, she preferred to work as the Lord had led her.

She was especially careful about selecting workers. That was one reason for the no-salary policy. Many Indians would have gladly been baptized and worked for the mission in order to make a living. "Guard your gate" was one of her favorite warnings, and she heeded it herself. Some of her friends and supporters often were surprised when she rejected applicants who, to them, seemed ideally suited for the ministry; but later events always proved her right. She prayed men and women into places of service, trusting the Lord to prepare them, provide for them, and protect them.

Protection was especially important, not only because of the Indian climate and unsanitary conditions, but even more because of the idolatry and demonism. Satan and his armies attacked the people and the ministry at Dohnavur in ways that make these experiences read like events from the Book of the Acts. The secret of victory? The Word of God and prayer!

Amma and her associates practiced John 15:7 and trusted God to guide them by the Word and provide for their needs a day at a time. I think it would be good for some of us to get acquainted with Amy Carmichael's principles for prayer: "(1) We don't need to explain to our Father things that are known to Him. (2) We don't need to press Him, as if we had to deal with an unwilling God. (3) We don't need to suggest to Him what to do, for He himself knows what to do." If all of us took these principles to heart, think of the religious speeches that would be silenced in many prayer meetings.

Amy Carmichael cautioned her helpers to "leave a margin" in their lives. We have all been reminded to "beware of the barrenness of a busy life." As I read Amy Carmichael's books, I am amazed at the broad scope of her reading, not only in many translations of the Bible, but in the mystics, the church fathers, even the Greek philosophers. To her, reading was an enriching experience, a time for relaxation and renewal and not just escape.

On October 24, 1931, Amy Carmichael suffered a serious fall, other complications set in, and she had to end her active ministry. She was limited physically to her room and an occasional veranda stroll, but that did not limit her ministry. In the next twenty years she wrote thirteen books and many letters, and she directed the work of the mission through her capable associates.

In 1948 she experienced a second fall, and from then until her Homegoing she was confined to her bed. But she was constantly at the throne of grace, and God answered her prayers. God is still answering those prayers, for the Dohnavur Fellowship continues to minister effectively in South India.

Amy Carmichael wrote thirty-five books of various kinds—the story of the Fellowship, poems, stories about the children who were rescued, devotionals, and messages for those who suffer. Many of them have been republished by Christian Literature Crusade and should be available in your local Christian bookstore. Not everyone takes to Miss Carmichael's writing; in fact, I must confess that it took me many years to learn to appreciate her style and message (*I* was the one who had to grow.).

His Thoughts Said . . . His Father Said is excellent for times of meditative pondering. *Thou Givest . . . They Gather* is another fine devotional book, compiled from her writings after her decease. Two encouraging books for people who suffer are *Candles in the Dark* and *Rose from Brier*. When *God's Missionary* was first published, it upset many people because of its emphasis on devotion and personal discipline. It still upsets readers—but perhaps they need to be upset. Books about Indian women reached through the Dohnavur ministry include *Mimosa, Ponnammal, Kohila,* and *Ploughed Under. Edges of His Ways* is a daily devotional book that is intellectually stimulating and spiritually rewarding.

"We were committed to things that we must not expect everyone to understand" was the way *Amma* explained her ministry and was also the reason why some devout evangelicals kept at a distance. "The work will never go deeper than we have gone ourselves" was her explanation of why some workers did not remain and why others refused to come. She did not try to please everybody or solicit anybody's support. The work was God's work, and he alone could prosper it. No high-powered machinery, no Madison Avenue promotion, no attempts to compete with other ministries either for funds or personnel.

Amy Carmichael depended on God for day-by-day and hour-by-hour direction. God spoke to her through the Word, through the pages of her dog-eared *Daily Light*, through the impulses of the heart; yes, on occasion, even through dreams. Seminary professors who write learned books about how to interpret the Bible would probably call her use of Bible texts or parts of texts superstitious; but they would have to confess that she was a woman led by God and blessed by God. She exercised a simplehearted faith in God, nurtured by a whole-hearted love for God; and her Father saw to it that she was cared for.

Here is a "Confession of Love" that she drew up for a group of Indian girls who banded together to serve Christ. Perhaps it says best to us just what Amy Carmichael believed about Christian life and service.

> *My Vow:* Whatsoever Thou sayest unto me, by Thy grace I will do it.
> *My Constraint:* Thy love, O Christ, my Lord.
> *My Confidence:* Thou art able to keep that which I have commited unto thee.
> *My Joy:* To do Thy will, O God.
> *My Discipline:* That which I would not choose, but which Thy love appoints.
> *My Prayer:* Conform my will to Thine.
> *My Motto:* Love to live—live to love.
> *My Portion:* The Lord is the portion of mine inheritance.

With that kind of devotion and dedication, is it any wonder that Amy Carmichael was misunderstood by believers, persecuted by unbelievers, attacked by Satan, and blessed by the Lord?

Unpredictable? Yes—*but not unblessable!* We could use a few more like her in Christian service today.

17

Jonathan Edwards—Brilliant Mind, Burning Heart

It is unfortunate that many people imagine Jonathan Edwards as a ranting Puritan preacher, pounding the pulpit and trying to frighten sinners into heaven. Of course, most of them have probably never read his famous sermon "Sinners in the Hands of an Angry God" or even examined the life of this godly man. For Jonathan Edwards was a quiet scholar, a loving father, a concerned pastor, and a man who loved God and longed more than anything else to glorify him.

Edwards was born into the home of Rev. Timothy Edwards at East Windsor, Connecticut, on October 5, 1703. He was the only son in the family; he had ten sisters. He came from good Puritan stock, especially on his mother's side of the family. Her father was Rev. Solomon Stoddard, revered pastor of the Congregational Church at Northampton, Massachusetts.

Stoddard was the accepted spiritual leader of the churches in the Connecticut Valley; in fact, some people called him "Pope" Stoddard. He pastored there for fifty years, and under his ministry there had been at least five special spiritual awakenings experienced.

Jonathan Edwards received his schooling at home; at an early age he learned Latin, and later he took on Greek and Hebrew. He had two passionate interests in those early years—science and religion. He watched the spiders and wrote an amazing essay about them. He saw the mind and heart of God in creation; everything in nature revealed to him something about God.

But his interest in spiritual things was remarkable for a boy so young. He prayed five times each day. With some of his friends he built a "booth" in the swamp, and there they used to gather together to discuss spiritual matters and to pray. I must confess that the boys' clubs my friends and I formed in our youthful years centered more around fun and games.

In 1716, when he was thirteen, Edwards entered Yale college, where he invested four years in undergraduate study and then two more years studying theology. It was while he was at Yale that he had two life-changing experiences. The first was his conversion when he was about seventeen years old. Since childhood he had revolted against the doctrine of the sovereignty of God. But as he read I Timothy 1:17, he had a remarkable experience of the sense of God's greatness and glory, and all his theological objections disappeared.

"As I read the words," he wrote in his personal account, "there came into my soul, and was as it were diffused through it, a sense of the glory of the divine Being; a new sense, quite different from anything I ever experienced before. . . . From about that time, I began to have a new kind of apprehensions and ideas of Christ, and the work of redemption, and the glorious way of salvation by Him."

Edwards was never content to have a book knowledge of God. He sought to experience God in his own life in a personal way. He was not an ivory-tower theologian, spinning webs of words. He always centered in on the experience of the heart; and it was this conviction that brought him many spiritual blessings as well as many spiritual battles.

His second crisis experience was more intellectual than spiritual, although Edwards would never divorce the mind and the heart. He read John Locke's *Essay Concerning Human Understanding* and made an about-face in his approach to the problem of how people think and learn. He came to the conclusion that "knowledge" was not something divorced from the rest of life but that a man's senses helped to teach him truth. In other words, sensory experience and thinking must go together. Again, Edwards saw the importance of uniting the mind and the heart.

This approach would govern his philosophy of preaching for the rest of his life. He would first aim for the heart and move the affections before trying to instruct the mind. In one of his most important books, *A Treatise Concerning Religious Affections*, Edwards wrote, "True religion, in great part, consists in holy affections." However, he opposed emotion for emotion's sake. He carefully explained the difference between shallow emotionalism and true affections that prepare the way for men and women to receive God's truth.

On January 12, 1723, Jonathan Edwards made a solemn dedication of himself to God. Earlier he had made a list of Resolutions, which he read once each week and sought to obey daily. From time to time, he added to this list as he saw special needs in his life. He used it, not as a law to bind him, but as a compass to guide him and a mirror to help him examine his progress in his spiritual walk.

On February 15, 1727, Jonathan Edwards was ordained and became assistant to his grandfather, Solomon Stoddard. On July 20 of that same year, he married Sarah Pierrepont, an exemplary Christian lady who bore him eleven children. It is worth noting that Jonathan Edwards used to spend at least one hour each evening with his children before they went to bed. He often studied thirteen hours a day, yet he took time for his family. He and his wife were very happy together; their marriage and their home were a testimony of the goodness and grace of God.

In February 1729, Solomon Stoddard died, and Jonathan Edwards became the pastor of the church, perhaps the most important congregation outside Boston. Spiritual life in the

American colonies was very low, and there was a desperate need for revival. Preachers were generally well-educated, but they lacked a burden for souls and power in preaching. Some of them were not even converted themselves!

"I am greatly persuaded," wrote George Whitefield when he visited New England, "that the generality of preachers talk of an unknown, unfelt Christ. And the reason why congregations have been so dead is because dead men preach to them."

But the preachers were not the only ones to blame. While the founders of the churches had, for the most part, been converted people who feared God, their children and grandchildren were too often unconverted but baptized church members.

The churches operated under what was known as the Half-Way Covenant. It permitted people to unite with the church if they had been baptized but had not made a profession of faith in Christ (they were baptized as infants, of course). Their children were then baptized as "half-way members," but they were not permitted to share the Lord's Supper or vote in church elections.

But Solomon Stoddard went even further in opening the doors of the church to unsaved people. He decided that the Lord's Supper was a saving ordinance and that unconverted people should not be barred from the table. The result, of course, was a church composed largely of unconverted people who gave lip service to the doctrine but who had never experienced the life of God in their own hearts.

Obviously the new pastor and his flock were on a collision course. Edwards had experienced eternal life in an overwhelmingly personal way. It was his conviction that truth must be experienced in the heart as well as understood in the mind. In his study of the Word, he concluded that church membership and the Lord's Supper were for saved people alone. He realized that many of the "children of the covenant" in the colonies were living in sin, apart from God, and destined for eternal destruction.

In 1734 he preached a series of sermons on justification by faith. The time was ripe, and the Spirit began to move. In the next year, Edwards saw more than three hundred people unite with the church. Some notable sinners in the town were converted, and some remarkable events took place. This was one of the early phases of a spiritual movement in America that historians call the Great Awakening, covering a period from about 1725 to 1760.

Whenever the Spirit works, the flesh and the devil start to work to counterfeit God's blessing; and it was not long before excesses appeared in the revival movement. George Whitefield had joined in the movement in 1740, and in some of his meetings people had fainted, cried out with fear, and even experienced fits of shaking. Whitefield, like Edwards, did not encourage these activities, but they had no control over them. Ministers who opposed religious enthusiasm openly criticized Edwards and accused him of leading the people astray; so Edwards wrote and published a book on how to discern a true working of God's Spirit, *The Distinguishing Marks of a Work of the Spirit of God*. It is still today one of the best studies of religious psychology available.

That same year (1741), Edwards was invited to preach at Enfield, Connecticut, and on July 8, he preached "Sinners in the Hands of an Angry God," perhaps the most famous sermon ever preached in America.

The text is Deuteronomy 32:35: "Their foot shall slide in due time." There is no question that Edwards had one purpose in mind: to shake the people out of their religious complacency and into the saving arms of the Lord. Edwards was always quiet in his delivery; he read from a manuscript and rarely looked at the people. He did not pound the pulpit or shout. He simply opened up the Scriptures and warned lost sinners to flee from the wrath to come.

The Spirit of God broke into the meeting, and many people came under conviction. Some cried out in fear. A minister sitting on the platform pulled at the preacher's coattails and said, "Mr. Edwards! Mr. Edwards! Is not God also a God of mercy!" Edwards had to stop preaching and wait for the congregation to become quiet. He concluded the sermon, led in prayer, and closed the meeting. Those who remained afterward to talk to the preacher were not necessarily upset or afraid. In fact, people were impressed with the cheerfulness and pleasantness of the expressions on faces.

Concerned with the salvation of the lost, Jonathan Edwards could not continue to live with the compromising situation that he had inherited at Northampton. In 1748, he informed the church that he would not receive as new members persons who had not given evidence of salvation, nor would he permit unconverted people to come to the Lord's Table. Even though ministers in that day had far more authority and respect than they do today, this step was daring and was violently opposed by most of the leaders in the church.

There followed nearly two years of debate and discussion, and the result was the dismissal of the pastor. Edwards preached his farewell sermon on July 1, 1750, a pastoral message that showed no animosity or bitterness, although certainly the preacher was a man with a broken heart. His text was II Corinthians 1:14, and his emphasis was on what would happen when ministers meet their congregations at the future judgment.

History has proved that Edwards was right and his congregation wrong. The colonial churches that rejected the working of God and refused to examine people as to their spiritual experience eventually turned from the faith and became liberal. The churches that followed Whitefield and Edwards continued to win the lost, send out missionaries, and train ministers who were true to the faith. An unconverted ministry and an unconverted membership are the devil's chief weapons to oppose the work of God.

Jonathan Edward moved his wife and large family to Stockbridge, Massachusetts, where he ministered as a missionary to the Indians. His income was reduced, of course, and yet God provided all their needs. Freed from pastoral duties and church problems, Edwards now had more time to study and write; during those Stockbridge years (1751–58) he wrote several of his most important works, some of which were published after his death. In 1757 he was named president of Princeton College, an office that his son-in-law Aaron Burr had held. He took office in 1758, when a smallpox epidemic was invading the area; he caught the infection through an innoculation that back-fired, and on March 22 he died.

We have had more than two hundred years to evaluate the life and ministry of Jonathan Edwards. He was perhaps the greatest thinker that America ever produced, and yet he had the heart of a child. He was a great theologian, and yet his books and sermons touch life and reach into the heart. He was the rare blend of a biblical scholar and revivalist. He had a longing to see people know God personally, but he refused to accommodate his theology just to get results. He was also a man concerned about missions. Even the *Encyclopaedia Britannica* admits, "By his writings and example, he gave impetus to the infant evangelical missionary movement."

Edwards was not afraid to give his people solid doctrine. His Resolution 28 reads: "Resolved to study the Scriptures so steadily, constantly and frequently, so that I may find, and plainly perceive myself to grow in the knowledge of the same." Some preachers today seem to have time for everything else but Bible study and the preparation of spiritual nourishment for their people. It is easy to borrow a sermon from a book, or to listen to another preacher's message on cassette.

Edwards used imagination in his preaching. Like every good teacher and preacher, he turned the ear into an eye and helped people to *see* spiritual truth. He knew that the mind is not a debating chamber; it is a picture gallery.

He was a courageous man who held to his biblical convictions even though it cost him his church and the loss of many friends. He stood with George Whitefield when many were opposing him. Edwards encouraged spiritual awakening even though he knew there would be excesses and abuses. He would have enjoyed Billy Sunday's reply to the critic who said that revivals did not last: "Neither does a bath," said Sunday, "but it's good to have one once in awhile!" He preached for decisions in an era when ministers were not supposed to disturb the congregation.

The Works of President Edwards (a single volume) may be available in your local library. Ola Elizabeth Winslow has written one of the best biographies, *Jonathan Edwards*, published by Macmillan in 1940. She also edited a helpful anthology of his most important sermons and writings, *Jonathan Edwards: Basic Writings* (New American Library).

Jonathan Edwards on Heaven and Hell by Dr. John Gerstner is a fascinating and very readable study of this important subject. It is published by Baker Book House. Dr. Gerstner is perhaps our leading evangelical scholar when it comes to the life and theology of Jonathan Edwards. For a satisfying but readable study of Edwards's theology, read *Jonathan Edwards, Theologian of the Heart,* by Harold Simonson (Eerdmans).

Our nation is desperately in need of spiritual awakening. But our emphasis on evangelism apart from doctrine will certainly not do it. The Great Awakening was the result of solid doctrinal preaching that addressed itself to both the heart and the mind. It was preaching that dared to expose sin in the church. And God used it to sweep thousands into his family.

Perhaps it is time that we dug again these old wells and learned why their waters flowed with life so fruitfully and so bountifully.

Samuel Chadwick— A Burning and Shining Light

Samuel Chadwick is not as well known as he deserves to be, and I propose to remedy that situation as best I can. I am amazed to discover that Chadwick is not named in either *The Wycliffe Biographical Dictionary of the Church* or the monumental *New International Dictionary of the Christian Church*, although the former finds room for the poet Chaucer, and the latter gives space to the English devotional writer Richard Challoner. I suspect that as an evangelist, educator, and editor, Samuel Chadwick did more to win the lost and to build the church than all the poets and devotional writers of his day.

He was born September 16, 1860, in a modest home in Burnsley, Lancashire, England. Burnsley was a mill town, and Chadwick said that "there was not a blade of grass, a tree, or a flower" in the area where he lived. "It would be difficult to imagine anything more drab, prosaic, and uninteresting than our street!"

At the age of eight, he went to work in the cotton mills, and thus developed the discipline of early rising, a practice he continued throughout his life. In later years he thanked God that he grew up among the laboring people, so that he might understand their needs and minister to them. At an early age he became interested in the political meetings, mainly because he enjoyed listening to the speakers. He used to read aloud the speeches of Gladstone and Disraeli as reported in the newspapers. Unconsciously, he was being prepared to become one of England's greatest preachers.

When he was ten years old, Chadwick was converted to Christ through the ministry of Samuel Coley, guest speaker at the Sunday school anniversary meeting. From the very beginning of his spiritual life, Chadwick began to emphasize prayer. "I went apart three times a day," he wrote, "and prayed in spirit all the time between. The habit of three times a day was not easy. The dinner hour was short, the family was large, and the house small, but I managed!"

In 1875, when he was fifteen years old, Chadwick felt a call to ministry, a decision he pondered and prayed about for a whole year. His resources were limited, his health was not good, and he had received little education. His family was poor and would not be able to send him to school. But he was determined to serve Christ; so after working twelve hours a day in the mill, he devoted five more hours to personal study at home.

The Methodist superintendent in the Burnsley Circuit, Josiah Mee, discovered Chadwick's desire to serve Christ and encouraged him to preach. Almost every Sunday he would walk to various preaching stations in the Methodist Circuit and share the Word of God. He enjoyed preaching, but for some reason he did not see any fruit from his ministry. It would be seven years before the Lord would reveal to him the secret of spiritual fruitfulness.

In 1881 Chadwick was appointed lay evangelist at nearby Stacksteads, a district saturated with open sin and opposition to the Gospel. Proud of his preaching ability and his file of sermons, the young evangelist went to work, but the forces of Satan were too much for him. He desperately needed power.

He banded together with a small group of burdened people and covenanted with them to pray daily for revival.

As Chadwick prayed, God dealt with him, particularly in the area of his pride. At three o'clock one Sunday morning, the young Methodist preacher burned all his sermon outlines and made a complete surrender to the Lord. That was the beginning of revival. At the early prayer meeting, he led his first soul to Jesus Christ. Before that Lord's Day ended, Chadwick led seven people to the Savior.

Sensitive to the Spirit's leading, Chadwick wisely suspended all the regular services of the church and called the congregation to prayer. Tuesday evening two women in the church, known to be enemies, patched up their differences and knelt together in prayer at the communion rail. Others joined them, and the Spirit began to move among the people. There was no excessive display of emotion, but everyone knew that God was in their midst.

The turning point came when the town drunkard, Robert Hamer, showed up at the meeting. He was known as "Bury Bob," and there was hardly a sin or crime that he had not been involved in one way or another. People had seen him eat glass, fight rats with his teeth, break furniture, swallow knives, and fight policemen. That night, he asked for a Band of Hope pledge card, signed his X, and vowed he would never drink again. The following Sunday Bury Bob was converted, and his life and home were so transformed that it led to the salvation of many others.

What the congregation did not know was that behind the scenes their youthful pastor had been praying that God would stir things up by converting some notorious sinner. Chadwick had been studying John 11 and 12 and had noticed that the resurrection of Lazarus had led to the conversion of many people. "That's the solution!" he said to himself. "We need a Lazarus!" God answered his prayers; Bury Bob was his Lazarus, raised from the dead and given new life in Jesus Christ. From that time on, in every church he pastored and evangelistic crusade he conducted, Samuel Chadwick asked God to give him a Lazarus.

"If God is at work week by week raising men from the dead," he said, "there will always be people coming to see how it is done. You cannot find an empty church that has *conversion* for its leading feature. Do you want to know how to fill empty Chapels? Here is the answer: Get your Lazarus."

From 1883 to 1886, Chadwick was a student at Disbury College, where he read every book he could secure and listened to the lectures as though his instructors were inspired apostles. It was his one opportunity for formal training, and he wanted to give his best to his Lord. His concern for lost souls and his unsophisticated ways bothered a few of the students and staff, but fortunately, his education did not put out the fire that God had ignited in his heart. "Passion does not compensate for ignorance," he used to say in later years. He was indeed a balanced man.

He ministered as an assistant pastor in Edinburgh for one year following graduation, and then as minister at the Clydebank Mission in Glasgow for three years. At Clydebank, he had a new building but no congregation; so he set out to win people to Christ and build his own church. He visited in homes, preached on the street corners, fought the brewers and gamblers and quickly assembled a band of men and women who loved the Lord and their young pastor.

One classic story must be repeated from those Glasgow days. The brewers had applied for five new licenses to put up pubs in strategic places, and Chadwick went to court to oppose them. The attorney for the brewers did his best to ridicule the young pastor, ending his speech with, "I should like to ask this young-looking shepherd, what hast thou done with the few sheep in the wilderness?"

Chadwick jumped to his feet and replied, "Don't you trouble about my sheep! I'm after the wolf today!"

In 1890, the Methodists officially ordained Samuel Chadwick and sent him to Wesley Chapel, Leeds, where he ministered for three years. He then went to London for a year, but in 1894 he was back in Leeds, this time at the prestigious (but spiritually dead) Oxford Place Chapel. For the rest of his life, he would be known as Chadwick of Leeds. He ministered there

for thirteen years and again saw miracles of grace in the lives
of sinners as he preached the Gospel of Jesus Christ.

"I saw at the table at my first Band Meeting," he reported,
"and listened to their doleful tales of difficulty and despair,
laughing at their fears. I knew no way of conducting a mission
except that of getting people saved." Within the first six months
God gave him not one Lazarus but half a dozen.

There was a strong agnostic movement in Britain at that
time, with Secularist Societies springing up in almost every
city. One Sunday evening, the entire Secularist Society of Leeds
filled the gallery of the church, hoping to disrupt the ministry.
But that night their leader was converted. And within the next
few weeks, every single officer in the group was won to Christ.

After thirteen fruitful years in Leeds, Chadwick accepted a
call to teach at Cliff College, the Methodist school in Sheffield,
Yorkshire. He promised them five years, but even while he was
teaching, he was busy holding evangelistic meetings and helping to establish missions in South Yorkshire. In 1913 Chadwick
was made principal of Cliff College and embarked on a program of training young people for ministry. For nearly twenty
years he taught students how to pray, depend on the Spirit,
preach the Gospel, and seek to win lost souls to Christ.

Chadwick was unique, and space does not permit retelling
all the stories that came out of his life and ministry, but here
are a few instances. There was the student who asked him for
permission to smoke his pipe, even though it was against the
rules. "I have been a smoker for twenty years," he argued,
"and I am just dying for a smoke!"

"Are you really dying for a smoke?" Chadwick asked.

"I am, Sir," the student replied.

"Then," said Chadwick, "sit down in that chair and die!"

Before long, the student was on his knees beside the principal, and God answered prayer. The boy was delivered from
the habit.

Then there was the time when a ministerial candidate was
almost rejected because he was short of stature. Chadwick
stood to his feet and protested. "The only fault the Committee

had to find with this candidate,"he said, "is that his legs are short; and I want to know how long this Conference has been measuring men at that end!"

When some of the "intellectual" young pastors tried to bring a "new gospel" into the Methodist movement, Chadwick opposed them. "Go down to the South Yorkshire coalfields and try your new gospel," he cried out at the conference, "and see what it will do. Until you have got a Gospel that works—shut up! This is not an age for twiddling your thumbs!"

Chadwick used to hold large anniversary services at Cliff College, and he always prayed for generous offerings to help the college. After one morning service, a guest gave him a large check and said, "I have been blessed this morning!" Chadwick took the check, lifted his eyes to heaven and prayed aloud, "Lord, bless him again tonight!"

Chadwick made seven visits to the United States and ministered at such important centers as D. L. Moody's Northfield and the Winona Lake Bible Conference. God used him to stir Christians to have a concern for the lost and a desire for holy living. For many years he was editor of *Joyful News*, the official publication of the Joyful News Mission, which eventually merged with the Wesleyan Home Mission Committee. His articles on prayer were published in book form in 1931 as *The Path of Prayer*. It is still one of the best books on the subject and has been reprinted by the Great Commission Prayer League (P.O. Box 360, Leesburg, Florida 32748).

The Way to Pentecost is another of Chadwick's books that has had a wide ministry. It was published by Hodder and Stoughton in London and is distributed in the United States by the Christian Literature Crusade. You need not agree with every detail of the author's theology to benefit from the insights and impact of this book. I especially appreciate his sane approach to the delicate subject of spiritual gifts. In his own inimitable way, Chadwick writes, "The Gift of Tongues comes last on the list, and is first in controversy!"

Before I leave Samuel Chadwick, I want to point out that he was a very close friend of Dr. G. Campbell Morgan. It is worth noting that Morgan also, in his early ministry, wrestled with pride of preaching and burned his sermon outlines. Like Chadwick, Morgan rose from obscurity to become one of England's greatest preachers and Bible teachers. In 1904, when Morgan was considering the call to Westminster Chapel, London, he had a long talk with his friend Chad before he made his decision. Chadwick wrote to Morgan when the Morgan family moved to America in 1919: "I cannot tell all your friendship has meant to me. I am flattered when people bracket my name with yours, and though I know the distance at which I follow, it pleases me that they think of us together. The privilege of your friendship I reckon among God's best gifts and my chiefest joy."

Chadwick served as president of the Methodist Conference in 1918 and president of the Free Church Council in 1922. In 1927 and again in 1930 he underwent serious surgery that left him quite weak, but he carried on as best he could in the strength of the Lord.

He died on Sunday, October 16, 1932, at the age of seventy-two, but before his Homegoing, he called his colleagues to his bedside and gave them a farewell message.

Stand together for the Word of God. . . . Stand in a spirit of unity, of faith, of doctrine, according to the fourth chapter of Ephesians. . . . I have stood true to the last. I have had no doubts. I have been sure of the Living God. He knows my limitations, but I have loved Him and trusted in His mercy. My ministry has been the message of the Cross.

A Methodist through and through, Samuel Chadwick belonged to the whole evangelical world because he preached the fundamentals of the faith and sought to bring sinners to the Savior. "The qualities of powerful personality," he said, "are courage, power, sympathy, and sanity." He possessed all of them and, yielded to the Spirit, gave himself to the greatest work in the world—the winning of lost souls to Jesus Christ.

19

Bishop with a Bible

"Beware of divisions. One thing the children of the world can always understand, if they do not understand doctrine; that thing is angry quarrelling and controversy. Be at peace among yourselves."

So wrote Bishop John Charles Ryle in his farewell message to the ministers of the Liverpool Diocese on February 1, 1900, as he closed nearly twenty years of faithful ministry among them. Four months later, on June 10, he died; but he left behind a spiritual legacy that has enriched believers and strengthened the church.

The Church of England, to which Ryle belonged, was not a united people. For years there had been a high-church faction that promoted ritual and always seemed to be drifting nearer to Rome; a broad-church group that was tolerant of diverse religious emphases but not too enthusiastic for the Gospel; and then the low-church segment, known also as the Evangelicals. It was to this latter group that Bishop Ryle belonged.

The Evangelicals in the Church of England grew out of the great revivals of Whitefield and Wesley. Converts who left the church and united with independent groups were called Methodists. But those who remained in the Anglican Church and were true to their doctrinal convictions were called Evangelicals, and they were a great and glorious host. Some of the greatest Gospel-preaching ministers in English church history were a part of the Evangelical movement—men like William Romaine, Henry Venn, Charles Simeon, William Grimshaw, John Fletcher, and John Newton, who wrote "Amazing Grace."

It was not easy to be an Evangelical in the Established Church. You would not be recognized by those in authority, and you would probably not be promoted or offered the better churches. The majority of the clergy endured the presence of the Evangelicals the way a fishing party endures gnats and mosquitoes, always hoping they will somehow go away. Evangelical clergy were not appointed to the boards of various church ministries or, for the most part, asked to preach at important church functions. But the Evangelicals practiced their faith and made a monumental contribution to both the church and the nation. It was the Evangelicals who led the fight against slavery, child labor, poor factory conditions, and the abuse of the poor and the insane. Much of what we value in modern social legislation, and perhaps take for granted, grew out of the ministry of Wesley and Whitefield and their successors.

The Evangelicals also founded a number of effective organizations to promote the spread of the Gospel: the Church Missionary Society (1799), Religious Tract Society (1799), British and Foreign Bible Society (1804), and several more. They had a burden for Israel and started a mission board for witness to the Jews. In both home and foreign missions, they led the way, seeking to win the lost and build new churches. They shocked their more proper brethren by daring to preach out of doors, as Jesus and Paul did. They even held evangelistic services in unconsecrated buildings. For all of this, of course, they were criticized; but their only concern was to please their Master, so they kept right on.

John Charles Ryle was born May 10, 1816, in Macclesfield, Cheshire, the center of the great silk industry in Britain. The Ryle family had long been established there and had been quite prosperous. Several of the men, including Ryle's father, had served as mayor. There was a strong Evangelical element in the family's faith, going all the way back to 1745, when John Wesley himself had preached in that region.

At the age of twelve, Ryle entered prep school, leaving in 1827 to enter Eton, from which he graduated in 1834. He then enrolled at Oxford, and the year in which he graduated (1837) he was soundly converted. His sister and a cousin had been converted earlier and had witnessed to him. A serious illness just before his final examinations also gave him time to reflect on his life and consider spiritual things.

He had attended one of the parish churches one Sunday afternoon, but neither the sermon nor the hymns made any impression on him. But when a man began to read the second Scripture lesson for the day, the Word gripped his heart. The passage was Ephesians 2, and when the reader got to verse 8, he read it with special emphasis: "For by grace are ye saved— through faith—and that not of yourselves—it is the gift of God." Young Ryle believed that word, and God saved him.

In preparation for sharing his father's banking business, Ryle studied law in London; but after six months, he had to return home because of ill health. However, he soon recovered and entered into business with enthusiasm. He was considered one of the most eligible bachelors in the district: young, popular, successful, and a devoted Christian. But he was afraid of women. His father offered him a free house and a large sum of money if he would marry, but even these incentives did not move him.

In June 1814, the bank failed, and the family lost everything. Ryle's father had followed some bad advice and had hired an untrustworthy manager; the combination of the two brought ruin. The family was left with Mrs. Ryle's dowry, some personal property, and their clothes. Mr. Ryle spent the next twenty years paying back every cent of the indebtedness, with each member of the family assisting in every way possible. Even when John was rector at Helmingham, he wore threadbare clothes in order to save money and assist his father. He firmly believed that his father's personal spiritual falling away was the real cause for the failure of the bank.

Before the year was over, young John determined that God had called him to the ministry. He was ordained December 12 and preached his first sermon December 19. He began his ministry at Exbury and then was appointed to Winchester, these brief experiences helping to prepare him for the longer ministries that were to follow. From 1844 to 1861, he served at Helmingham, where he had a rather difficult time with the lord of the manor, who tried to run both the town and the church. Ryle went through the valley during those years, burying his wife of less than two years in 1847 and his second wife in 1860.

From 1861 to 1880, Ryle ministered at Stradbroke, and during that time he met and married his third wife. These were happier years. For one thing, there was no rich landlord to throw his weight around; and, for another, his people loved him and were eager to hear the Word preached. He led them in the physical restoration of the old church, making certain that the pulpit was given its proper place of prominence. He had the workmen carve on the pulpit "Woe is unto me if I preach not the Gospel!" When the workmen had finished, he took a tool and underlined the word "not" with a deep groove.

In 1880, John Charles Ryle was appointed the first Bishop of Liverpool, a new diocese that had been carved out of the Chester diocese. How did it happen that an Evangelical was appointed to this important position and given the opportunity to build an Evangelical ministry from the ground up? From the human point of view, the appointment may have been just a piece of religious politics; but God certainly overruled it for the good of his church.

At the February 1880, election, Prime Minister Benjamin Disraeli suffered an overwhelming defeat at the hand of Gladstone. Disraeli was anxious that a staunch Protestant be appointed to the new post, and the leading churchmen of Liverpool were behind him. The fact that Liverpool was Gladstone's hometown made Disraeli's decision even more significant. Ryle was given a very little time to consider the offer because time was working against them; so he immediately accepted, and three days before Gladstone took office, all the formalities had been completed.

On May 4, Oxford University conferred the Doctor of Divinity degree on him, and on June 11, he was consecrated bishop. It is doubtful that Ryle would ever have been considered for the post had he not proved himself to be a sane, spiritual Evangelical who was willing to listen to those he disagreed with and ignore those who threw stones of accusation from the fringes of the camp. Ryle let it be known from the beginning where he stood on the great doctrines of the faith; but he also made it clear that he was going to use his new position to promote harmony, not conflict, in the church.

One of Ryle's first tasks was to build a ministry there in Liverpool, and this he did, gathering around him like-minded Christians who wanted to share the gospel and build churches. Instead of raising money to construct an ornate cathedral, Ryle used the funds available to extend the church. He built ninety places of worship and staffed them with 136 ministers. He established a ministry of "Bible women" to assist the resident clergy and to take the Gospel to the poor. He organized ministries for children and even used secular buildings for religious services. He was too conservative for the liberals and too liberal for the ultra conservatives, so he was attacked from both sides. But valiantly he carried on a positive ministry, never dishonoring the Savior or diluting the doctrines of the Reformed faith. Before long, the church life in the diocese began to take on a new spirit of excitement, and God began to bless.

Always a man with a great heart, Ryle saw nothing wrong in cooperating with the Nonconformists, including D. L. Moody and Ira Sankey when they came to Liverpool in 1883. His friendly attitude toward the Methodists rankled some of the more exclusive Anglican clergy, but their criticisms did not disturb him.

On February 1, 1900, Bishop Ryle resigned from his charge.

He had lived to see nearly one-fourth of the parishes in his diocese staffed by Evangelicals. When he was buried in Liverpool, his old Bible was placed in his hand in the coffin. Two texts were quoted on his gravestone: Ephesians 2:8 and II Timothy 4:7, which states, "I have fought a good fight, I have finished my course, I have kept the faith."

Baker Book House has reprinted a number of Bishop Ryle's books, including his monumental *Expository Thoughts on the Gospels*, a set that ought to be in every Bible student's library. *The Best of J. C. Ryle* is a good sampler for the reader not yet acquainted with this giant of the faith. His books on *Holiness*, *The New Birth*, and *Call to Prayer*, deal with essentials of the Christian life. *The True Christian* is a collection of Ryle's sermons on many subjects that relate to the Christian life.

Ryle was always a true son of the church, but he took a very definite Evangelical interpretation of the Thirty-Nine Articles of the Church of England. He explains his position in *Knots Untied*, published by James Clarke.

Banner of Truth Trust, London, has reprinted *Warnings to the Churches*, a series of addresses that focus primarily on the church and its ministry (several of these chapters also appear in *Knots Untied*). Ryle's biographical studies, *Five Christian Leaders* and *Five English Reformers*, are also available from Banner of Truth.

Ryle's successor, Bishop Chavasses, started the construction of the Liverpool Cathedral, with the laying of the foundation stone by King Edward VII in 1904. Queen Elizabeth II shared in the service of dedication when the building was completed, October 25, 1978. It is a beautiful sandstone building, and my wife and I visited it a few years ago. It was the south choir aisle I was especially interested in, for in that aisle is a monument to the glory of God and the honor of his servant, Bishop John Charles Ryle. However, his greatest monument is not man-made. It is in the *living* church, in the lives of men and women who even today are touched by his ministry.

"I am firmly persuaded," he wrote, "that there is no system so life-giving, so calculated to awaken the sleeping, lead on the inquiring, and build up the saints, as that system which is called the *Evangelical* system of Christianity. Wherever it is faithfully preached, and efficiently carried out, and consistently adorned by the lives of its professors, it is the power of God. . . .

"We have the truth, and we need not be afraid to say so."